Online Resources

Access pre-made smart contracts as part of the online resources. These smart contracts will help you implement your learnings in the real world and give you an in-depth understanding of the concepts. The templates include:

- IdentityVerification.sol: Smart contract that can be used to verify identification

- RealEstate.sol: A smart contract that keeps track of the ownership in real estate

- Voting.sol: A smart contract that can be used for voting purposes

- ShipmentTracking.sol: Contract to track the shipment from the owner to the current location

- SimpleToken.sol: A smart contract that represents a basic token on the Ethereum blockchain

- Simple.sol: A basic smart contract that stores a message onto a blockchain and also has functions to retrieve the same message.

To access the templates, follow the steps below:

1. Scan this QR code to land on the product page

2. Request the online resources by filling in the required details.

bit.ly/blockchain-slm

Happy self-learning!

This page is intentionally left blank

SELF-LEARNING MANAGEMENT SERIES

VIBRANT
PUBLISHERS

BLOCKCHAIN ESSENTIALS

YOU ALWAYS WANTED TO KNOW

From Basics to Real-World Applications

DR. ABHILASH KANCHARLA

Blockchain Essentials You Always Wanted To Know

First Edition

Paperback ISBN 10: 1-63651-300-X
Paperback ISBN 13: 978-1-63651-300-3

Ebook ISBN 10: 1-63651-301-8
Ebook ISBN 13: 978-1-63651-301-0

Hardback ISBN 10: 1-63651-302-6
Hardback ISBN 13: 978-1-63651-302-7

Library of Congress Control Number: 2024946692

This publication is designed to provide accurate and authoritative information in regard to the subject matter covered. The Author has made every effort in the preparation of this book to ensure the accuracy of the information. However, information in this book is sold without warranty either expressed or implied. The Author or the Publisher will not be liable for any damages caused or alleged to be caused either directly or indirectly by this book.

Vibrant Publishers books are available at special quantity discount for sales promotions, or for use in corporate training programs. For more information please write to bulkorders@vibrantpublishers.com

Please email feedback / corrections (technical, grammatical or spelling) to spellerrors@vibrantpublishers.com

To access the complete catalogue of Vibrant Publishers, visit www.vibrantpublishers.com

This book is dedicated to my grandmother, whose wisdom, resilience, kindness, and lessons on the importance of family are invaluable principles I carry with me that have shaped my life in countless ways. Thank you for your unwavering love and for being my greatest teacher.

About the Author

Dr. Abhilash Kancharla is an Assistant Teaching Professor in the Computer Science department at The University of Tampa, teaching undergraduate-level courses. Before his teaching at The University of Tampa, Dr. Kancharla also taught Computer Science courses at Oklahoma State University, where he received his Master's and Doctorate degrees in the same field. Dr. Kancharla started his career as a software tester at Capgemini while working for clients like HSBC, Capital One, and Bank of America. He has worked for over five years with blockchain, primarily Ethereum and Hyperledger blockchains. His work involved modifying the Ethereum source code for better performance and scalability. Dr. Kancharla also works as an ad-hoc reviewer for blockchain and queueing-related papers at MDPI Journal. He has organized two workshops at IEEE that are related to blockchain, incorporating the concepts of AI and NFT. His secondary area of research consists of works related to Big Data and Hadoop. He also received his ISTQB certification as a software tester.

SELF-LEARNING MANAGEMENT SERIES

TITLE	PAPERBACK* ISBN
ACCOUNTING, FINANCE & ECONOMICS	
COST ACCOUNTING AND MANAGEMENT ESSENTIALS	9781636511030
FINANCIAL ACCOUNTING ESSENTIALS	9781636510972
FINANCIAL MANAGEMENT ESSENTIALS	9781636511009
MACROECONOMICS ESSENTIALS	9781636511818
MICROECONOMICS ESSENTIALS	9781636511153
PERSONAL FINANCE ESSENTIALS	9781636511849
PRINCIPLES OF ECONOMICS ESSENTIALS	9781636512334
COMPUTER SCIENCE	
BLOCKCHAIN ESSENTIALS	9781636513003
DATA ANALYTICS ESSENTIALS	9781636511184
PYTHON ESSENTIALS	9781636512938
ENTREPRENEURSHIP & STRATEGY	
BUSINESS COMMUNICATION ESSENTIALS	9781636511634
BUSINESS PLAN ESSENTIALS	9781636511214
BUSINESS STRATEGY ESSENTIALS	9781949395778
ENTREPRENEURSHIP ESSENTIALS	9781636511603
GENERAL MANAGEMENT	
BUSINESS LAW ESSENTIALS	9781636511702
DECISION MAKING ESSENTIALS	9781636510026
INDIA'S ROAD TO TRANSFORMATION: WHY LEADERSHIP MATTERS	9781636512273
LEADERSHIP ESSENTIALS	9781636510316
PRINCIPLES OF MANAGEMENT ESSENTIALS	9781636511542
TIME MANAGEMENT ESSENTIALS	9781636511665

*Also available in Hardback & Ebook formats

SELF-LEARNING MANAGEMENT SERIES

TITLE	PAPERBACK* ISBN

HUMAN RESOURCE MANAGEMENT

TITLE	PAPERBACK* ISBN
DIVERSITY, EQUITY, AND INCLUSION ESSENTIALS	9781636512976
DIVERSITY IN THE WORKPLACE ESSENTIALS	9781636511122
HR ANALYTICS ESSENTIALS	9781636510347
HUMAN RESOURCE MANAGEMENT ESSENTIALS	9781949395839
ORGANIZATIONAL BEHAVIOR ESSENTIALS	9781636510378
ORGANIZATIONAL DEVELOPMENT ESSENTIALS	9781636511481

MARKETING & SALES MANAGEMENT

TITLE	PAPERBACK* ISBN
DIGITAL MARKETING ESSENTIALS	9781949395747
MARKETING MANAGEMENT ESSENTIALS	9781636511783
SALES MANAGEMENT ESSENTIALS	9781636510743
SERVICES MARKETING ESSENTIALS	9781636511733
SOCIAL MEDIA MARKETING ESSENTIALS	9781636512181

OPERATIONS & PROJECT MANAGEMENT

TITLE	PAPERBACK* ISBN
AGILE ESSENTIALS	9781636510057
OPERATIONS & SUPPLY CHAIN MANAGEMENT ESSENTIALS	9781949395242
PROJECT MANAGEMENT ESSENTIALS	9781636510712
STAKEHOLDER ENGAGEMENT ESSENTIALS	9781636511511

*Also available in Hardback & Ebook formats

Table of Contents

What experts say about this book!

As a blockchain expert, I am thoroughly impressed by the remarkable depth and accessibility of this book. Tailored for graduates and professionals in both tech and management, it strikes the perfect balance between being highly informative and exceptionally easy to understand.

The book's organization, from foundational concepts in "Chain of Blocks!" to the forward-thinking discussions in "The Future of Blockchain", ensures a comprehensive learning journey. Complex topics like cryptography, smart contracts, and blockchain integration are broken down in an approachable manner, making them accessible even to those new to the field. Yet, the advanced discussions on Hyperledger, decentralized networks, and case studies ensure that even seasoned professionals will gain invaluable insights.

What truly stands out is the book's practical approach. The chapters on tools like Truffle and Ganache, as well as hands-on guidance for writing smart contracts, provide real-world applicability. The inclusion of quizzes and chapter summaries further reinforces learning, making this an ideal resource for academic, professional, or personal development.

Whether you are a technologist looking to deepen your understanding, a manager seeking to implement blockchain solutions, or a student stepping into this exciting field, this book is a must-have. I highly recommend it for its clarity, thoroughness, and vision.

– Melissa Amouny,
Blockchain and DeFi Specialist,
Researcher & Consultant

Preface

I started my journey with blockchain in 2016, coinciding with the flourishing time period of blockchain. Before that, I had been working on distributed databases (Hadoop), which eventually helped me understand blockchain a little better.

Every semester, I introduce myself to the students of my class in the first lecture. Given that I have worked on blockchain and still am working, I bring up blockchain to see how many of them have had exposure to that term before. It's usually a handful of them who have encountered blockchain. As soon as I shift that question to a more familiar one — How many of you have heard of Bitcoin before? Quite often, the answer to that question is — almost everyone. The unfamiliarity surrounding the foundational technology of cryptocurrencies is one of the main reasons I decided to write this book.

This book stems from my deep-rooted connection with blockchain over the last seven years. It is targeted at beginners, enthusiasts, and individuals who have heard the term blockchain before, but seek a comprehensive understanding of its intricacies.

Upon completing this book, I hope you gain a fundamental grasp of the inner workings of blockchain. It's important to understand that this book doesn't give you any financial advice on investing in cryptocurrencies. By the end, you will have the knowledge to appreciate the impact blockchain is currently creating and will continue to create in society.

Most of all, I hope you find this book useful and occasionally entertaining.

Introduction to the book

Welcome to Blockchain Essentials You Always Wanted To Know! Blockchain has received the most attention during the last decade in terms of popularity among both tech and finance enthusiasts. If you haven't heard the term "Blockchain", that's most likely because it was overshadowed by the names of cryptocurrencies – Bitcoin, Ethereum, Ripple, and many more. Blockchain is the technology that drives cryptocurrencies as we know them today. It is only recently that additional use cases have been developed for blockchain, other than just using it for cryptocurrencies. Some of the use cases comprise using blockchain technology in voting, healthcare systems, supply chains, NFT, real estate, etc. Right now, blockchain technology is considered a practical substitution in almost every domain. Just like how the internet made a sensation in the 90s, blockchain is also poised to make a big impact in the future, on both the technological and financial side of a wide range of markets and industries for the ad-hoc uses mentioned earlier.

This book has been designed to help you understand the underlying fundamentals of blockchain. The book also talks about how and why blockchains have become popular. In the later chapters, the book also goes a little technical by creating a simple blockchain and smart contracts. That being said, if you already know what a blockchain is and have worked with blockchain before, this book might not be right for you, as it is aimed at users who are traversing for the first time into the waters of blockchain.

The book uses Ethereum architecture to explain the technical concepts of blockchain. These concepts can be applied to architectures that have a close resemblance to Ethereum's. Each chapter starts with learning objectives and within each chapter you can find sections named Fun facts, New Terms So Far, Words of Caution and Tips. Finally, each chapter concludes with a summary and multiple-choice questions to test your understanding.

Expectations and Results

There is no expectation about your background in finance, economics, or computer programming. But, it does assume that you are familiar with being able to perform simple tasks on a computer, which will come in handy for Chapter 5. The simple tasks range from opening files, editing text files, installing/uninstalling application software, navigating through the folders in your computer, opening certain programs and so on.

By the time you reach the end of this book, you will be able to:

- Understand the basic concepts of how blockchains work

- Understand the various vocabulary surrounding blockchain

- Learn and explain the different types of blockchains

- Create a simple Ethereum-based blockchain on a private network

- Program a smart contract and deploy it on the blockchain

- Learn different use cases of blockchain

- Explore various case studies involving blockchain projects

- Grasp the future of blockchain

Note

Unfortunately, this book doesn't provide any financial advice on cryptocurrencies or investments related to cryptocurrencies. The focus of this book revolves around the basics of blockchain technology (underlying architecture that runs cryptocurrencies), by providing essential concepts, systems, architecture, and networks of blockchain.

How to use this book?

Welcome to the blockchain guide, designed for readers with little to no prior knowledge of the subject.

1. Start by immersing yourself in the foundational chapters that explain the fundamental concepts of blockchain technology. As you progress, pay attention to real-world examples and case studies that illustrate the practical applications of blockchain. If you are just starting to get to know blockchain, I highly suggest going through the entire book from start to finish.

2. Take advantage of clear and concise explanations, accompanied by illustrations and analogies, to grasp complex ideas easily.

3. Whether you're a curious beginner or someone looking to deepen your understanding of blockchain, this book aims to demystify the technology. As blockchain continues to redefine industries and reshape our digital future, staying informed will be essential, considering the rapid pace at which this transformative technology evolves.

4. If you are keen on learning to program in blockchain, Chapters can be read in this order - 1 -> 2 -> 5 -> 6 -> 4 -> 3 -> 7. On the other hand, if you are more interested in the theoretical foundation of blockchain, chapters can be read from 1 to 7, skipping chapter 5.

5. In this book, you are going to find some new terms that you will need to read to understand what I'm trying to get across. Undoubtedly, blockchain is a young concept

that goes hand in hand with other much younger concepts so it's not possible to cover every term for every concept that is brought in here, but because I know that these terms are new and they will be used throughout the book, I will mention them as we go, with a brief explanation. An asterisk (*) will be used when these terms appear in the sentence, superscripting the word (for example, transaction*). You can look at the "New Terms So Far" section to read their definition and a short comment on what it means.

6. Keep an eye out for words/phrases that are superscripted by a pound symbol (#). For example, web3#. These words indicate that there's additional information or interesting insights in the "Fun Facts" section that immediately follows the occurrence of that word in the text.

Who can benefit from this book?

This book will benefit you if:

1. You have little or no prior understanding of blockchain technology

2. You are an entrepreneur exploring innovative solutions

3. You are a student eager to delve into emerging technologies

4. You are a professional seeking to navigate the impact of blockchain on your respective industry

5. You are a curious person intrigued by the decentralized landscape of blockchain

This page is intentionally left blank

Chapter 1

Chain of Blocks!

This book will start by introducing the definition of blockchain along with the most common terminologies that revolve around blockchain architecture. We will then look into the history of blockchain followed by some common use cases for it. Currently, blockchain technology and architecture are being explored as use cases in various fields such as blockchain-based healthcare, financial services, gaming, AI/ML (Artificial Intelligence/Machine Learning), IoT (Internet of Things), security, etc. Later on, we will also look into why blockchain has gained huge popularity in recent years. We will then get to the conclusion by talking about what is "Web3", a term that was coined based on blockchain.

After studying this chapter, you should be able to:

- Define blockchain in your own words

- Explain the contents of a blockchain in general

- Outline the basic structure of blockchain

- Understand the history of blockchain

- Give a list of possible use cases for blockchain

- Describe blockchain-related terms like Web3, Web2, and P2P

1.1 Definition

The simplest definition of blockchain is evident from its name itself – "BLOCK-CHAIN" — a chain of blocks, as the title of this chapter suggests, but that is not a good enough definition of blockchain to understand everything about it. So before we get into the formal definition of blockchain, here is an example of what a blockchain will look like using a real-world analogy. That way, when we are looking at the formal definition, it will help you easily visualize its concept.

One of the closest and simplest representations of the logical structure of blockchain is that of a goods/freight train as shown in Figure 1.1. A goods train will usually have one engine at its head and wagons attached one after another. Sometimes, a long goods train might have multiple engines attached at the head or even an engine attached at the tail, but in our case, we will assume that the train has only one engine. Each wagon in the train is connected to its previous one, except for the head which is the starting point.

Another assumption we will make about the train is that you cannot unlink a wagon in the middle. If one of the wagons in the middle needs to be replaced or removed, all the wagons behind it must be removed one by one to accommodate the replacement.

To be more precise, if there are 50 wagons attached to the train and the 23rd wagon from the engine has to be replaced, then all the wagons have to be detached one by one from the tail-end until we reach the desired wagon to be replaced. The closer the wagon to be replaced is to the engine, the harder and more time-consuming it will be to change that wagon. That being said, we are also assuming that the wagons cannot be removed from the end where the engine is located and the wagons are always removed at the tail end. In short, removing/replacing a wagon closer to the tail-end is a lot easier and less time-consuming than replacing a wagon closer to the engine.

| Figure 1.1 | A locomotive is the closest example to visualize the structure of blockchain. |

Now that you can visualize the blockchain# structure, let's dive into a more formal definition. *A blockchain is a data structure* that consists of a monotonically increasing* list of records called blocks which are connected in the form of a chain.*[1] These so-

1. Nakamoto, Satoshi. (2009). Bitcoin: A Peer-to-Peer Electronic Cash System. https://bitcoin.org/bitcoin.pdf

called blocks are, in turn, linked to each other with cryptographic algorithms that hold the blocks in place, just like how a hook holds all the wagons in place for a freight train. The linking of the blocks in the blockchain is done using cryptography* and we cannot see the link/chain physically. The links are made in such a way that it will be tough (but not impossible) to change the contents of the existing blockchain. Technically, once a block is attached to the blockchain, the contents of the block cannot be modified. There are some exceptions to this immutability feature, which we will talk about in detail in the further chapters.

Every so often, a new block is created and linked to a "chain" of previously created blocks. The time intervals in which the new blocks are added is blockchain-dependent. The more the blocks attached to the blockchain, the bigger the size of the blockchain. A block is analogous to a wagon in the train, just like how a wagon can contain multiple items within it, a block can also consist of one or more transactions*/records. On a similar note, an engine located at the front of the freight train is analogous to the first block in the blockchain. The first block is often referred to as the *genesis block*[2]. Newly formed blocks are consecutively added one after another.

The contents of the block include various items ranging from transactions, timestamps, hash values and so on. A transaction/s is added to the block and the block gets added to the blockchain eventually. Any user on the network can create a transaction and add it to the block. The complexities of creating, verifying, and adding a transaction will be discussed eventually in the later chapters.

---

2. The term Genesis block was not used in the Bitcoin paper, but rather was introduced in the Bitcoin's software code and documentation.

From the definition of blockchain provided above, we know that it is a data structure, but more importantly, the data structure is distributed, implying that there is no central authority in the blockchain system. Blockchains use distributed application architecture — P2P. P2P, short for Peer-to-Peer, is a distributed architecture that spreads the workloads among equally privileged peers, with no central authority managing the flow of data (Sections 3.1 and 3.2 cover P2P in detail). Peers in the blockchain, more often referred to as *nodes*, adhere to a consensus* algorithm to append new blocks. Consensus in simple terms means everyone agrees on the same thing. The consensus algorithm used depends on the architecture of the blockchain. No matter what kind of consensus algorithm is used, the primary goal of consensus will be to validate new transactions that are added to the blockchain. One of the original consensus algorithms is derived from the solution to a famous problem called the "Byzantine Generals Problem". Consensus algorithms are discussed in detail in Chapter 3.

Figure 1.2   Basic architecture of blockchain

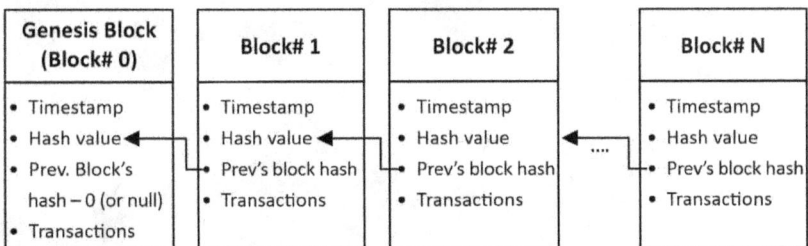

Genesis Block (Block# 0)	Block# 1	Block# 2	Block# N
• Timestamp • Hash value • Prev. Block's hash – 0 (or null) • Transactions	• Timestamp • Hash value • Prev's block hash • Transactions	• Timestamp • Hash value • Prev's block hash • Transactions	• Timestamp • Hash value • Prev's block hash • Transactions

By looking at Figure 1.2 (depicting the architecture of blockchain) and Figure 1.1 (a freight train), we can come to the conclusion that both structures resemble each other. In fact, in computing terms, the essential component of the blockchain structure that connects all the blocks is referred to as a *Merkle*

tree*. In future chapters, we will dive much deeper as to why it's hard to modify a blockchain and how a Merkle tree is formed along with more insights on the tree data structure.

It's been only a few pages so far, and yet there were many new terms used, along with a lot of unanswered questions like:

How are blocks formed?

What are transactions?

What cryptographic algorithms are used to append blocks together?

Why are we talking about Greek generals in a technology book?

What is a Merkle tree?

What is the main purpose of blockchain?

Where can I buy fruits from Merkle trees?

What does a goods train carry?

Aaaah! So many questions! All of these questions will be answered in the upcoming chapters one by one, except for the last two.

Fun Fact

While blockchain first earned a wide audience in 2008, the story of blockchain itself starts in 1982, when David Chaum published a dissertation that described a blockchain-like architecture under the title *Computer Systems Established, Maintained, and Trusted by Mutually Suspicious Groups*.[3] Later, in 1991, a series of works by Stuart Haber and W. Scott Stornetta[4] proposed ways of keeping records that made tampering with document timestamps impossible, which in blockchain terminology means that one can't tamper with the timestamps of transactions.

New terms so far

- **Data structure:** A data structure is a group of data values, where there is a relationship or interaction taking place between them. A data structure is used to:

  - hold or store data.

  - organize data.

  - process data

  - retrieve data

  On the other hand, There are various data structures, some of which are designed for a specific purpose. Merkle tree is one such data structure and unfortunately, it's not a tree that gives fruits!

3. David Lee Chaum, Computer Systems Established, Maintained and Trusted by Mutually Suspicious Groups, University of California, Berkeley, 1982

4. S. Haber, W.S. Stornetta, "How to time-stamp a digital document," In Journal of Cryptology, vol 3, no 2, pages 99-111, 1991.

- **Monotonically increasing:** Always increasing or remaining constant, and never decreasing. Implying that a blockchain will always increase when new blocks are added or remain the same when no activity is happening.

  - **Strictly increasing:** Always increasing and never decreasing or remaining constant. For example, the age of any creature is always strictly increasing.

- **Cryptography:** A discipline dealing with techniques for securing information and communication from unauthorized disclosure (especially in military communications) based on mathematical reasoning. Generally speaking, Cryptography is the art and science of constructing and analyzing techniques for keeping messages secure from third parties or the general public.

- **Transaction:** An agreement signed off between a buyer and a seller to give goods, services or financial assets in exchange for money. The transaction is the meat of a blockchain, and contains everything about the respective addresses (not avenues!) of sender and receiver(s), time stamps, value of the transaction, and more. The contents of a transaction are somewhat variable from blockchain to blockchain.

- **Merkle tree:** Another name for a hash tree, a way of allowing you to know your order has been verified by the ledger without having to download all the previous blocks/transactions on the blockchain.

- **Consensus:** In common terms, they refer to a compromise, a concurrence of opinion or decision by a group of individuals. In the context of blockchain or distributed systems, consensus means there is a complete agreement about some piece of information or state between all the computers or nodes in a network.

1.2 History of Blockchain

Developed by a person (or group of persons) known by the name Satoshi Nakamoto and first announced on a mailing list in October 2008, Blockchain was intended to eliminate the need for a trusted third party for online financial transactions by utilising a peer-to-peer (P2P) network. "A purely peer-to-peer version of electronic cash would allow online payments to be sent directly from one party to another without going through financial institution." Satoshi Nakamoto (5 April 1975[#]) is a name used by the presumably pseudonymous individual(s) who created Bitcoin, authored the Bitcoin white paper, developed and deployed Bitcoin's original reference implementation, based on previous work by Stuart Haber, W. Scott Stornetta and Dave Bayer. There have been many claims as to the identity of Nakamoto, but these claims are unverified. At this point in time, and at the time of publication of this book, the identity of Satoshi Nakamoto remains unknown. The Bitcoin white paper can be found at www.bitcoin.org/bitcoin.pdf. The first cryptocurrency Bitcoin became very popular in 2010-2011.

This is the typical flow of a financial transaction outside the blockchain: To send money outside the blockchain, you walk into a bank and say: "I want to send $50 to my friend". The bank checks that you really have $50 in your account. Once checked, the bank puts the $50 in your friend's account, while at the same time removing $50 from your account. In this process, the bank acts as a third party to verify that you indeed sent money to your friend. The reason why Nakamoto invented blockchain is to remove the third party between two users who are exchanging money. Instead, Satoshi wanted funds to be exchanged from one user to another directly without the help of any interference. In a blockchain, you can simply send money to your friend without any banks. Along with the motivation of getting rid of third parties for fund transfer, Bitcoin also aimed to prevent the double-spending problem of money without any intervention.

Fun Fact

How do we know when Satoshi was born if we never got to know his actual identity? Satoshi Nakamoto originally published the paper on a public forum called p2pFoundation, where they listed their birthdate as 5th April 1975.

1.3 Use Cases of Blockchain

The previous section has introduced blockchain very briefly, and while the use cases of blockchain are talked about in much detail in the upcoming chapters, here is a glimpse of places where blockchain can be a great addition/replacement. Blockchain was primarily designed for one task — to be able to exchange finances (cryptocurrencies like Bitcoin). Several other cryptocurrencies have emerged after blockchain gained popularity. Some of the prominent ones include – Bitcoin (BTC), Ethereum (ETH), Binance Smart Chain (BSC), Cardano (ADA), Solana (SOL), Polkadot (DOT), Avalanche (AVAX), Tezos (XTZ) and many more. Not all the new blockchains that were developed solely focused on the financial nature of blockchain. Several blockchains shifted the focus from cryptocurrencies to utilizing the idea of smart contracts. This emergence of smart contracts within the blockchain architecture has resulted in the proliferation of diverse use cases for blockchain technology. Some of the scenarios where blockchain could make a potential fit are listed below:

1.3.1 Smart contracts

These are computer programs encoded to trigger events and actions when the contract's terms dictate. When the contract terms are met, smart contracts will allow the data to be permanently placed on a blockchain and executed automatically. The vast majority of the use cases listed below can be achieved only through the use of smart contracts. That is to say that blockchain by itself without smart contracts will achieve only one use case, and that is the ability to record and transfer digital value from one account to the next. By the end of this book, you too can create a smart contract and publish it to a blockchain to be executed whenever the contract terms are met.

1.3.2 Healthcare

In the realm of healthcare, blockchain technology offers a robust solution for managing medical records and health information. This innovation can be used by healthcare professionals worldwide, thus removing the physical boundaries of medicine by facilitating seamless access to patient data for healthcare professionals worldwide. Health data that is stored on a blockchain is almost always carefully structured to not include personal health information on the blockchain directly but in the "off chain" space around it. Remember, the blockchain is a distributed ledger, where every interaction or "block" entered is visible to each participant. Alternatively, in some cases, a private blockchain may be employed to restrict access to authorized parties only.

1.3.3 Supply chain and logistics

With the help of blockchain in the supply chain industry, we will be able to track the items from the manufacturing point to the final destination i.e., supply chain companies can document production updates to a single shared ledger* which provides complete data visibility. The transferability of the product manufacturing not only helps companies trace the product but also improves trust between the customer and the seller. It would give the end customer a great deal of satisfaction to know where the product that was purchased came from.

1.3.4 Property and real estate

With the help of smart contracts, transferring real estate ownership can be done with ease. The records of real estate are stored/monitored in the blockchain and will be visible to anyone connected to the blockchain, thereby adding transparency in the transition of ownership for property and real estate.

1.3.5 Finance

The most basic use of blockchain is to transfer digital money to other parties without the intervention of third-party services like banks. This was the very first use case of blockchain (Bitcoin cryptocurrency). Blockchain allows cross-border payments regardless of the location with the transaction fees being much less on average compared to banks.

1.3.6 NFT marketplaces

Some of the more prominent recent applications of blockchain involve non-fungible tokens* (NFTs) that track and assign rights to the ownership of a wide array of assets, from the simple ones (images) to the more complex (items in a video game). In either case, NFTs create or "mint" the particular asset and smart contracts are fundamental to the process of automatically assigning rights to ownership of the token.

1.3.7 Government

Almost instantaneous cryptocurrency payments can help the government provide foreign aid, which usually is a nightmare given the checklist and the approvals to be done by third-party financial institutions, especially when every country has its laws to abide by. Using blockchain, third parties can be removed from e-government services, which eventually reduces corruption in these industries

1.3.8 Voting

Blockchain has the potential to make the voting process secure. Voter fraud can be minimized to zero as blockchain will help invalidate duplicate votes. Using blockchain as a voting platform gives complete transparency over the results of the election not only to the government but also to the people. This transparency of voting procedures can result in increased trust in the government too.

1.3.9 IoT

IoT stands for Internet of Things and means connecting sensors that are embedded in everyday objects that can then communicate with and send data over the Internet or other communication networks. You might, for instance, use blockchains to authenticate the communication between sensors because it would enable the exchanged data to be checked by the entire (distributed) network that manages the chain. For example, imagine a weather channel equipped with sensors distributed worldwide. By utilizing blockchain technology, the channel can verify that the data received from these sensors remains untampered with.

1.3.10 Gaming

Some contemporary video games incorporate elements that utilize blockchain technologies, such as cryptocurrencies and NFTs, wherein players can buy, sell, or trade items that they acquire through gameplay with other players. In such scenarios, the game publisher makes money by charging fees for every transaction. Often, this requires players to use tokens to buy in-game items or currency (for instance, an NFT that could naturally increase the value of that token).

1.3.11 Personal identity security

Although the idea of using blockchain for personal security doesn't go along with each other because blockchains are public, there are some scenarios related to identity/security where blockchain would be the correct fit. IBM has developed digital credentials based on blockchain technology, aiming to create tamper-proof identities that serve as verifiable credentials, streamlining credential management for both individuals and organizations.

1.4 What Made Blockchain So Popular?

The following section tries to answer the question — Why has blockchain become the buzzword in the last few years and since when did it get so popular? There are quite a few reasons why blockchain gained so much popularity in recent years. One such reason for the popularity of blockchain is the return on investment (ROI) one could get in cryptocurrency. Up until this point, the only use for blockchain was the transfer of funds. Fast forwarding a few years after the founding of Bitcoin, the people who built the Ethereum blockchain came up with the concept of smart contracts. This idea revolutionized the blockchain industry by bringing about many different use cases apart from just cryptocurrency.

Fun Fact

The price of one Bitcoin around 2010 was 10 cents. If you had purchased a dollar worth of bitcoins at that time, then you would have had roughly 10 bitcoins. If the same 10 bitcoins were sold back in November of 2021 (which was the peak of bitcoin price to date), you could have cashed out approximately $680,000. From investing $1 in 2010 to cashing out $680,000 11 years later is mind-boggling; the interest rate in this case would be 2300% per year! Before 2010, there was a time when the price of Bitcoin was as low as $0.0009 per bitcoin.

Now that we have a better picture of the use cases of blockchain in brief, the remaining section describes a few more features of blockchain that made it as popular as it is today:

1.4.1 Cryptographically secure

Cryptographically secure is the process of applying a digital signature to create and post a transaction which helps validate that the transaction originated from the sender and is not a counterfeit. On top of that, the data structure technically used by blockchain is called a Merkle tree and this also makes the chain irreversibly secure. The use of Merkle trees in blockchain makes it very difficult to alter the contents of the transactions without the change getting notified to other users of the blockchain.

1.4.2 Transparency

All the information stored in blockchain in the form of various transactions is immutably recorded and is time- and date-stamped, providing full transparency. This enables anyone connected to the blockchain to view the entire history of the transaction, thereby eliminating any fraud or even third-party involvement. This feature of blockchain is very helpful, especially in use cases like supply chain, where the end-user will have a clear picture and be able to track a product from source to destination.

1.4.3 Automation

Smart contracts help us achieve the process of automation in blockchain. These contracts, written once, can be used to automate events and actions that take place under certain conditions. A well-written smart contract can not only reduce the paperwork but also prevent fraud and counterfeiting.

1.4.4 Exclusion of third-party services

While transferring funds/currency to another user on the blockchain, third-party services are not needed. For example, to transfer money to your friend, you and your friend should have some sort of bank account – which is a third-party service and the bank will possibly charge some fees for the transfer. The fees charged depend on different federal laws, on whether the transactions are made out of the border or transactions are made between two different banks. Many such rules and regulations determine the fees charged for transactions made by financial institutions. However, for blockchain, funds can be transferred without any intervention from third-party services.

An important point to note is that all the above four features of blockchain are not purely advantageous. We will see in the final chapter that some of these features also prove to be disadvantageous in a way.

1.5 Web3

Blockchain technology is at a stage that is comparable to where the Internet was 20 years ago. Indeed, blockchain (as a technology) was so novel that this technology is termed Web3. Web3 is the future of the internet, a web in which users have a greater level of agency over their private and public information on the web – who sees it, how it's utilized, and ultimately, who owns it. If you are thinking: "Surely there are Web2 rules and Web1 rules?" You're exactly right! Web2 (also known as Web 2.0) is a type of worldwide website that highlights user-generated content, usability, and interoperability aspects for end users.

Web 1.0 refers to the evolution of the first stage of the World Wide Web, which is characterized by simple websites that are pretty much static (in simple terms – just text). The static web pages at the time of Web1 were more like informational pages that didn't have any interaction with the user but rather, were only used to convey information. Web3 is a concept that includes some unique terms such as decentralization, blockchain technologies, and token-based economics. The first two Web evolutions focussed on – Hypertext: HTML*, HTTP*, and URI*.

We will dive deeper into Web3 in this section and revisit the concept of Web3 when introducing smart contracts in Chapter 5. It took more than 10 years for Web1 to evolve into Web2 and it's predicted that it might take even longer for everything in Web2 to evolve into Web3.

> **Fun Fact**
>
> Web3, also known as Web3.0, was coined by Polkadot founder and Ethereum co-founder Gavin Wood in 2014, roughly six years after the founding of Bitcoin. This term refers to a "decentralized online ecosystem based on blockchain". As a matter of fact, Web3 is one of the commands used in the Ethereum blockchain.

Web1 later transitioned to Web2 in the late 90s and hit its peak in the early 21st century. The transition happened due to the increased programming languages, skills, and techniques that the new programming languages allowed to perform. With the increase in the connection speeds of the internet and the intent of giving more control/access to the end-user, Web2 became popular. A more precise comparison could be made by likening Web 2.0 to a collaborative bulletin board or a community noticeboard. Here, users can post information, share updates, and engage with one another. This analogy more effectively conveys the concept of user-generated content and collaboration inherent in Web 2.0. Social media sites like Orkut, Facebook, Twitter, and Yahoo Messenger were some of the byproducts of Web2 technologies, enabling users of the web to communicate, share, and consume data.

Many websites and nearly all applications in the Web 2.0 era rely on some form of centralized database to deliver data and help enable functionality. For example, all the data about your Gmail information becomes part of Google's data centers/servers located around the world. If you want to see where exactly all the Google data centers are located across the planet, head to this link – https://www.google.com/about/datacenters. The underlying idea of Web 3.0 is to move away from the control of some central party or subject any web process to more than one single point of failure. So, in a blockchain, no information becomes part of one single point or place but exists as a copy on all devices that are interconnected in the blockchain.

New terms so far

- **Ledger:** A ledger, serving as a record book where transactions or important information are recorded and kept, is a shared and synchronized database across multiple participants, such as blockchain. It can be either private or public. Everyone involved with it possesses an identical copy of the ledger. Any changes made to the ledger are propagated to all connected users. This ensures that there is no risk of a single point of failure while simultaneously maintaining transparency in the records.

- **Token:** A token represents the set of rules encoded in a smart contract. A crypto token is a virtual currency, most often representing a tradable asset that resides in its own blockchain. There are different types of tokens in the blockchain world. Detailed explanations of tokens are provided in future chapters.

- **HTML:** HTML, short for Hypertext Markup Language, is the language that makes up most of the web, where HTML documents describe web pages. In contrast to a programming language, markup languages consist of a collection of elements or tags that describe what is contained on a webpage, such as a heading, a paragraph, an image, a link to another page, a bullet point, and so forth. Web browsers, such as Chrome, Firefox, Edge or Opera, will render (or display) the HTML tags as text and images in the format specified by the HTML to allow the user to interact smoothly.

- **HTTP:** Short for Hypertext Transfer Protocol, an application layer that makes use of the underlying data communication infrastructure that powers the World Wide Web. The hypertext documents include hyperlinks to other resources that the user can easily access, for example, by a mouse click or by tapping the screen in a web browser. The mouse click could perform operations like going to a new page, downloading an image, playing/pausing a video, and much more. All these activities are possible with the HTTP protocol.

- **URI:** An abbreviation for Uniform Resource Indicator, it is a unique sequence of characters used to identify a resource by web technologies. URI can be used to identify anything — people, items in video games, blockchain addresses, information resources, etc.

Key-Terms

Bitcoin	Block	Blockchain	Cryptocurrency
Genesis block	IoT	Merkle tree	Satoshi Nakamoto
Smart contract	Token	Transaction	Web1
Web2	Web3		

Quiz

1. **The technology that is used to link the blocks in a blockchain together is called:**

   a. Cryptography

   b. Linking

   c. Artificial Intelligence

   d. Mathematics

2. **Blockchain is used for:**

   a. Healthcare

   b. Supply chain

   c. Cryptocurrency

   d. All of the above

3. **Which of the following is an accurate representation that can be used to define a node in a blockchain?**

   a. Cryptocurrencies like Bitcoin and Ethereum

   b. An exchange where cryptocurrency can be purchased

   c. A computer connected to the blockchain network

   d. A blockchain

4. **Although the identity of the inventor of Bitcoin is not known to this day, what is the pseudonym for the inventor of Bitcoin?**

   a. Dave Kruger

   b. Satoshi Nakamoto

   c. Bitcoin

   d. Gavin Wood

5. **Which of the following options best describes a blockchain?**

   a. A distributed ledger on a P2P network

   b. A type of cryptocurrency

   c. Smart contracts

   d. Centralized database

6. **Considering that Bitcoin is a cryptocurrency, would it be accurate to say that it represents an application of blockchain technology?**

   a. True

   b. False

7. **Blockchain keeps a record of all the transactions made; these transactions can be recorded onto the blockchain _____.**

   a. without the involvement of a third party

   b. with the involvement of a third party

   c. without involving anyone authenticated

   d. with sharing passwords

8. Considering the transitioning of the web from Web 1.0 to Web 2.0 and then to Web 3.0, blockchain will fall under which category of web evolution?

   a. Web 1.0

   b. Web 2.0

   c. Web 3.0

   d. Blockchain is not considered a web technology

9. Which cryptocurrency's founder is responsible for coining the term Web3, the same term that is also used as a command in the platform's development and technology?

   a. Ripple

   b. Bitcoin

   c. Ethereum

   d. Blockchain

10. What does IoT stand for?

   a. Internet of Tasks

   b. Internet of Things

   c. Induction of Tasks

   d. Introduction of Things

Answers	1 – a	2 – d	3 – c	4 – b	5 – a
	6 – a	7 – a	8 – c	9 – c	10 – b

Chapter Summary

◆ Blockchain is a data structure in which a monotonically increasing list of records, AKA blocks, are connected together.

◆ Blockchain was initially created in 2008 by a person (or persons) who programmed under the name, or pseudonym, Satoshi Nakamoto.

◆ Blockchain is a technology that leverages the concept of working with distributed ledgers.

◆ Funds can be transferred on a blockchain without the intervention of third-party users.

◆ Smart contracts, healthcare, supply chain, real estate, IoT, gaming, and personal identity are a few use cases of blockchain.

◆ For every node in blockchain to be able to talk to every other node, blockchain relies on P2P services.

This page is intentionally left blank

Chapter **2**

Going Deeper into Blockchain

In the initial chapter, we explored the definition of blockchain and briefly examined its historical context. Having gained an understanding of blockchain's definition and background, this chapter will dive deeper into its underlying architecture, as well as examine the components of a block and a transaction. By the end of this chapter, we will have addressed topics such as how blocks are added, who is responsible for adding them to the blockchain, and the structural organization of a blockchain.

After completing this chapter, you should be able to:

- Explain the working architecture of blockchain

- Understand the difference between private and public key

- Describe the meaning of a digital signature

- Understand the key working mechanisms of blockchain including mining and consensus
- Describe the different types of consensus algorithms
- Understand the contents of a block and a transaction

2.1 Basics of Cryptography*

Before diving into the intricacies of blockchain's structure and formation, we will examine the cryptographic techniques employed within blockchain to safeguard user privacy and guarantee secure transactions. Cryptography encompasses the practice and study of methods for maintaining secure communication amidst potential adversarial actions.[5] This will allow only the sender and the intended recipient (receiver) to receive the messages and view their contents securely. With cryptography, you can be sure that the message you received from someone else over the blockchain is not altered by a third party. Modern cryptography can usually be classified into three categories:

- **Secret Key Cryptography:** This cryptography technique uses only one key to encrypt the data. Someone who is at the other end of the sender and receiver will be using the same key to decrypt the information. This is the oldest of all the three types of cryptography. For example, let's say you want to send a secret message to your friend using secret key cryptography. You both agree on a secret key beforehand. You use that key to encrypt your message and,

5. F. Piper, "Basic principles of cryptography," IEE Colloquium on Public Uses of Cryptography, London, UK, 1996, pp. 2/1-2/3, doi: 10.1049/ic:19960519.

when your friend receives it, he uses that same secret key to decrypt it and find out the original message.

- **Public Key Cryptography:** This is the kind of cryptography used for websites: encryption of data happens using a private key, with decryption via a public key. Visualise a mailbox with two slots: one where you post things and one where you're supposed to pick up what you've posted. The slot for sending messages is like your public key—it's open for anyone to drop a letter into. However, only you have the key to open the receiving slot, which is like your private key.

- **Hash Functions:** This form of cryptography is irreversible and is also used in blockchain in the form of Merkle trees. Hashing is a way to transform any amount of information into a fixed-length string[#]. The hash function is a versatile one-way cryptographic algorithm that maps any size to an output of a fixed length of bits, the number of bits depending on the hash algorithm used. The only way to decrypt the hash is to try all possible input combinations, which is why this form of cryptography is essentially irreversible.

In the field of computer science, the techniques used in cryptography are derived from mathematical concepts and a set of rule-based calculations called algorithms. This allows the messages from the sender to be transformed in ways that are hard to decipher. These deterministic algorithms are used for cryptographic key generation, banking transactions cards, computer passwords, e-commerce transactions, digital signing, verification to protect data privacy, web browsing on the internet, and even on your instant messaging services like WhatsApp, Snapchat, and so on.

Fun Fact

Cryptography was being used well before computers were invented. The oldest use of various cryptographic algorithms dates back to 1900 BCE. Some of the famous cryptographic algorithms since then are – Transposition Cipher, Caesar Cipher, Atbash, etc. With the computational power we have these days, most of these outdated ciphers can be backtracked. Caesar cipher is named after Julius Caesar who used a variation of this encryption around 100 BCE to send secret messages to his generals posted on the war front.

The following message doesn't look like it has any meaning:

LVYMUMRKSX SC PEX

However, what if I told you that the above message was encrypted using the Caesar cipher with a shift key of 10? The Caesar cipher (or Caesar shift or Caesar code) is a classic and simple cipher in cryptography. It comes under the umbrella of substitution ciphers, in which each letter in the plaintext is shifted by a certain number of places forward or backward in the alphabet. This shift is typically a fixed number, known as the "key" or "shift value." If the shift number is known, the message can be decrypted to get the real message. Below is the ROT-10 (short for "rotate by 10 places") table, that will help us decode the above encrypted message. For example, the last word PEX, can be decoded back to a meaningful word by substituting the appropriate letter from the table. PEX → FUN

Figure 2.1 ROT-10 lookup table for decoding/encoding using Caesar shift

A	B	C	D	E	F	G	H	I	J	K	L	M	N	O	P	Q	R	S	T	U	V	W	X	Y	Z
K	L	M	N	O	P	Q	R	S	T	U	V	W	X	Y	Z	A	B	C	D	E	F	G	H	I	J

On a similar note, the original message after decrypting should read:

BLOCKCHAIN IS FUN

2.2 Digital Signature, Private, and Public Keys

Recall from the above section that blockchain relies on hash functions and public-key cryptography. In a blockchain, those two building blocks work together to verify transactions between any two nodes in a blockchain network. Using the concept of cryptography, the science of encrypting, blockchains add the essential feature of immutability.

2.2.1 Digital signature

Digital signatures are typically used to confirm who you are; they are employed to tell other people that you are indeed the author of some digital message or transaction. Some additional content is tacked onto the message to prove that the message is coming from you as opposed to some imposter trying to act on your behalf. When you write out a cheque made out to a payee, you sign the instrument on the back so that the bank has some hard evidence that this signature was indeed produced by you. Thus, identity is confirmed by you being able to authorise a transaction. Pen-and-paper signatures are easy to forge, but not so easy when it comes to dealing with electronic signatures.

Before the document is sent, the sender generates a hash of the document from this information, which is a fixed-length string resulting from the unique content of the document. Then, the sender encrypts the document using the private key. Finally, the document is sent and, when received, the receiver can verify that it came from the sender by decrypting it using the shared sender public key. Digital signing is used by blockchain to show that the denominated sender indeed sent the transaction instead of someone else. Anyone with the sender's public key can decrypt the transaction to confirm its authenticity. This way the sender can prove to the entire network that the transaction was made by themselves.

Let's try to understand the idea of digital signature using a real-life example.

Let's assume Alice has indeed sent a transaction to Bob. If Alice signed the digital version of the transaction with her private key before sending it, Bob can check the digital signature to be sure that the transaction he received is exactly the same transaction that Alice sent. If the transaction was not signed by the appropriate private key before Alice sent it, Bob has no way of knowing that the transaction was unchanged – he has no way of knowing that Alice sent the transaction at all, in fact. Since there are no other services on blockchain, digital signatures have to be given priority, so that a receiver can be absolutely certain that the sender did indeed initiate a transaction, creating trust for Alice and Bob.

2.2.2 Private and public keys

Public-key cryptography entrusted to blockchain is an important part of the blockchain framework. This form of cryptography generates a pair of cryptographic keys, one public and one private. The private one is used to sign digital transactions that, more often than not, are used to send funds from one party to another.

The constraints of private and public keys might vary from one blockchain* to another. In Ethereum, a private key is a 64-character hexadecimal# address# that is used to digitally sign a transaction, thereby proving the ownership of funds used in a transaction. A private key should never be shared with anyone else. A private key once lost can never be recovered and all the funds linked to that account are lost as well.

On the other hand, a public key in an Ethereum blockchain[6] is a 42-character hexadecimal address derived from the last 20 bytes of the public key controlling the account with 0x# appended in front. An example of a public key would look like this –

0X370F497BCD1265F7A963D4D3E9C757DFDC43860B

A public key is an address to which anybody can send anybody money. If Alice is supposed to send Bob some crypto, Alice needs to be connected to the blockchain and in possession of her private key. But she also must know Bob's public address to initiate the transaction. There exists other ways to send crypto rather than by connecting to the blockchain itself. The simplest of these is using a crypto exchange that enables transfers on the (same or different) blockchain.

6. Vitalik Buterin, "Ethereum Whitepaper," Ethereum, accessed September 8, 2024, https://ethereum.org/whitepaper.

Caution

A private key can be used to produce a public key, but not the other way around – a private key cannot, for example, be generated from its corresponding public key. For this reason you need to keep your private key very safe. Correspondingly, since a public key cannot be used to produce a private key, it can be shared safely – but if you lose your private key there is no way to get it back.

New terms so far

- **String:** Unlike in real life, where a string is defined as a material consisting of threads of cotton or any such fabric woven together, in computer science, a string is a sequence of characters. Characters can be letters, numbers, symbols, or any other printable or non-printable characters, such as whitespace or newline characters. The text in computer programs is represented as a string. For example, "hello, world!", "12345", and "abc123" are all examples of strings. In the context of hashing, a string would be composed of 0 - 9 and A - F alphabets.

- **Deterministic:** In computer jargon, "deterministic" means that it will give you the same output in response to the same input. If you have a recipe for pancakes, it will give you the same pancakes each time if you use the same recipe and perform the same steps with the same ingredients. No randomness will be involved in this case, like dice-throwing.

- **Hexadecimal:** Just as the decimal using digits has a base value of 10, Hexadecimal numbers have a base value of 16. The total number of characters that a hexadecimal system can consist of is 16:

  1. Numbers from 0 to 9 account for 10 characters.

  2. And we use alphabets to stand for numbers from 10 to 15: 10=A, 11=B and so on up to 15=F, which is 6 more characters.

- **Address:** An address is a unique identifier that represents either a source or destination for cryptocurrency transactions, akin to an account number in traditional banking systems. Cryptocurrency addresses are usually derived from public keys through a series of mathematical operations. The public key is derived from the private key in a cryptographic operation, and then an address is derived from the public key. Putting it in simple terms, a bitcoin address is a mailbox and you can receive or send cryptocurrencies to a cryptocurrency address.

- **0X:** In computer science,"0x" or "0X" at the beginning of a string usually means that we are dealing with a hexadecimal (base-16) number or value. Since all public and private keys are hexadecimal, they are preceded by "0x". Note that "0x" itself is not part of the public/private key, it's a representation to denote the hexadecimal nature of the strings.

- **Adversarial:** Involving two parties who conflict with each other. Various cryptography algorithms focus on reducing adversarial behavior by implementing security which can be checked for authenticity on both ends.

A cryptographic adversary is someone who is
intentionally malicious and is trying to foil the users of
the cryptographic system. The cryptographic adversary
is trying to undermine the integrity of the blockchain by
attempting to alter the blockchain and to get the entire
ecosystem to believe it is the correct blockchain.

Fun Fact

The whitepaper by Satoshi Nakamoto describing
Bitcoin never mentions the word blockchain. It
describes the words "chain" and "block" but not
"blockchain" as a whole word.

2.3 Merkle Tree

To recap, Blockchain has blocks that are being held together
with cryptographic algorithms. This is achieved using the concept
of Merkle tree[7] to build blocks and thereby attach the blocks to
the blockchain one after another. We'll first take a moment to
define the building block of a Merkle tree, namely what a tree
is in the mathematical sense of the word, before diving into the
use cases, and advantages. A tree, in this context, is a hierarchical
data structure consisting of nodes linked by edges. It starts with
a single node called the "root," and each node can have zero or
more child nodes, forming a branching structure. The bottommost
nodes are referred to as the leaf nodes. There are various tree

---

7. Merkle R. Secrecy, authentication, and public key systems. Electrical Engineering,
PhD Thesis, Stanford University, 1979.

data structures and one of the simplest of all is called the binary tree and is shown in Figure 2.2. In a binary tree, each node is connected to at most 2 children nodes (left and right). To get an idea as to why these data structures are called trees, look at Figure 2.2 by flipping the book 180° - Doesn't that look like a tree?

Now, that we have an idea as to what a tree structure might look like, a node in a tree falls under any of the three types mentioned below:

- **Root node:** The topmost node in the tree, also often referred to as root. A root node does not have any parent above itself.

- **Leaf nodes:** A node in a data structure that does not have any children. The items at the bottom of the trees are coined as leaf nodes.

- **Non-leaf nodes:** All the nodes between the root node and the leaf nodes fall under the category of non-leaf nodes.

Figure 2.2 **Binary tree example with height# of 2.**

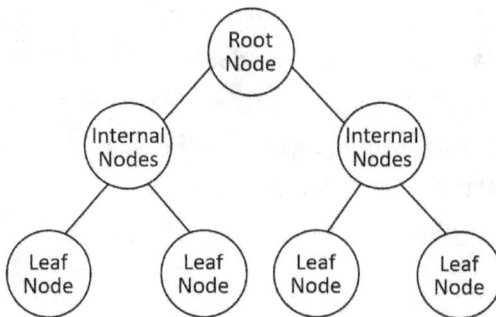

Trees are usually constructed top-to-down, but for a Merkle tree, we'll make the tree bottom-to-top, starting with the leaf nodes first. Every leaf node is annotated with exactly one cryptographic hash, and every non-leaf node is annotated cryptographically with a hash of two child nodes. Small changes to any part of the contents of any node anywhere under the Merkle tree will mean that the root hash at the top of the tree will not match with the original tree's root hash. The hash is an object of 256 bits, or 32 bytes and a unique signature for a text. The hash algorithm used in blockchain is the Merkle tree, called SHA-256. When the SHA-256 algorithm is given an input, it produces a set of 256-bit signatures that is almost unique. Given the same input, the SHA-256 algorithm will give an output that does not change, no matter how many times it is run, implying that a SHA-256 algorithm is deterministic. If the input is changed slightly, SHA-256 will create a completely new output.

The following example demonstrates the working algorithm of SHA-256:

The output of the SHA-256 algorithm on an input text of **"Blockchain Essentials"** was **"8db8ab48806cdb4a8305800a716ec24 3d983f8eb5b3f2 45d3034361c a15b547a"**. In fact, if you change anything at all in the input, you get a completely different output.

Take, for example, a second input text for our **"Blockchain essentials"**: **71adc8f7b0976592cc8d60839bfbf955952d3ae8 e2eed55 9740ba609f7c0412b**. Notice how dissimilar both outputs are when compared with each other (except for the fact that in one of the distinct inputs, the only difference being the word "essentials" has its first letter capitalised).

2.4 Working of Merkle Trees

The Merkle tree sums up all the transaction IDs in a block,

producing a "hash" (digital fingerprint) of the entire collection of transactions – and a transaction ID from the block can be verified to be in it. Any alteration in the block or its contents will instantly be apparent through the reconstruction of the Merkle tree for the block. If a new node is created on the blockchain then it must store a full copy of it locally. One must first verify the locally downloaded copy of the blockchain to ensure that the blockchain has not been tampered with. Data integrity of the blockchain can be checked by applying the Merkle trees algorithm.

Caution

The term "node" being used in this topic is not the same as the "node" used in other sections. Nodes in Merkle trees (or any data structure) represent some piece of information, whereas "nodes" in blockchain refer to the devices that are connected to the blockchain network. In this book, the term "nodes" are used in both contexts.

The following is the process involved in the creation of Merkle trees:

- Merkle trees are built from the bottom up using the transaction IDs that make up the leaf nodes of the tree.

- Using the SHA-256 hashing algorithm, two transaction IDs are combined and hashed together to form a new hash, which will represent a new non-leaf node.

- Once all the leaf node pairs are hashed, two non-leaf nodes are then combined and hashed to form a new level of hashes. Starting at the level of a leaf-node in a Merkle tree, the higher we go the lesser the number of hashes as each level decreases the number of hashes by at least 2 times.

- Merkle trees are made by hashing pairs of nodes repeatedly until only one hash remains. The nodes that are being referred to here are the transactions.

Figure 2.3 represents an idea of how the Merkle tree is used in blockchain. Consider a scenario where four transactions are supposed to be added into a block, namely - Tx_1, Tx_2, Tx_3, and Tx_4. At this point, we will not concern ourselves with what is present within the transactions themselves. Each transaction is individually hashed – meaning that regardless of the content of the individual transaction, a fixed-length string is obtained for all four transactions. The fixed length hash is represented by H_1, H_2, H_3, and H_4 in Figure 2.3. In turn, the obtained hashes are then again processed through the hashing algorithm such that two nodes are combined to form a fixed-length hash. This hashing process repeats until there is one node at the top.

Figure 2.3 **Merkle tree formation for four transactions**

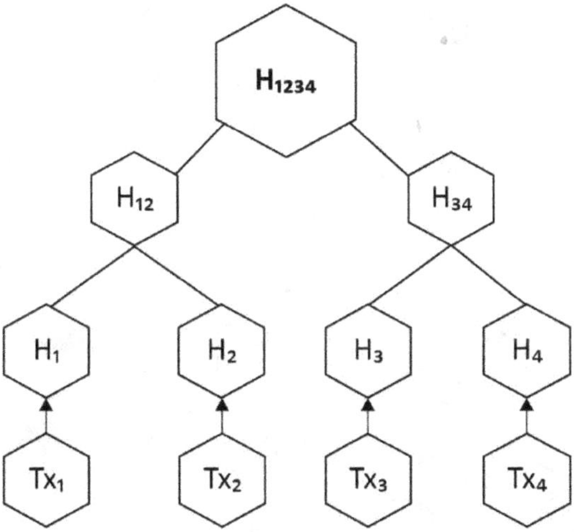

After looking at the picture, you are probably wondering – what if the number of transactions present in the block is not in powers of 2? For the above example we constructed a Merkle tree from 4 inputs (4 transactions as the leaf nodes) that would completely fill a perfect Merkle tree. Merkle trees formed will be perfect and symmetrical, as long as the number of leaf nodes are powers of 2 (2, 4, 8, 16 … 2^n and so on..). What if we have an odd number of actual transactions to be included? Then, in that case, the Merkle tree formed will not end up with a perfectly balanced-looking tree. There is nothing to worry about if the number of transactions is in odd numbers in any row or if the number of transactions is not a perfect power of 2. There are several ways to resolve this issue and this issue is handled differently with different blockchains. One way of creating a Merkle tree with five transactions is shown in Figure 2.4.

Figure 2.4   **Merkle tree with an odd number of leaf nodes**

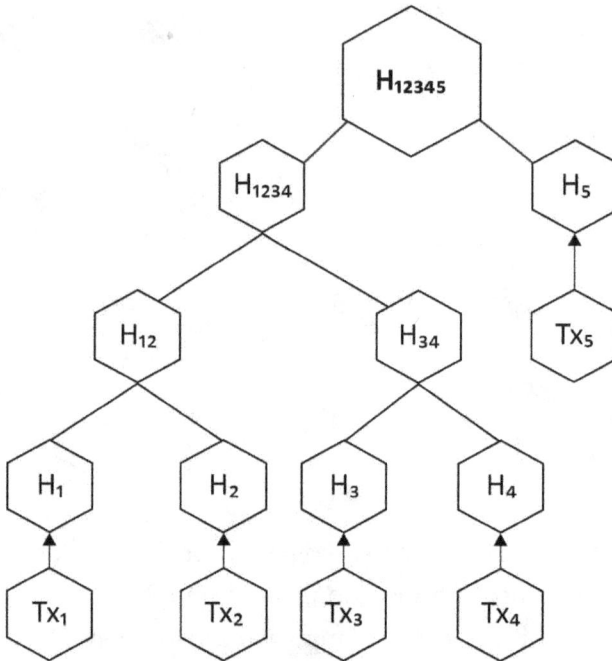

Fun Fact

Merkle tree is named after the computer scientist and mathematician Ralph C. Merkle. He also invented public-key cryptography and cryptographic hashing in the late 1970s. All these three algorithms are being used in blockchain and before using in blockchain, these algorithms have contributed significantly to the development of secure communication protocols on the internet!

2.5 Benefits of Merkle Trees in Blockchain

If there are no Merkle trees present in a blockchain, every copy of the blockchain on a node could be altered and there would not be a definite copy of the blockchain anywhere in the network. The data integrity[8] would be completely lost. The benefits of including Merkle trees are:

- Without Merkle trees, every node in the blockchain would be forced to keep a copy of the entire blockchain. Instead, a node can contain only necessary hashes essential to validate the Merkle trees.

- Merkle trees are one of the most efficient data structures to validate the integrity of data in general.

- Not only will Merkle trees be able to identify if there is a change made to the contents of the blockchain, but with proper application of Merkle trees, one can pinpoint the exact error too.

- The hashes generated by Merkle trees cannot be reverse-engineered easily as they use the SHA[#]-256 hash algorithm.

8. R. Kalis and A. Belloum, "Validating Data Integrity with Blockchain," 2018 IEEE International Conference on Cloud Computing Technology and Science (CloudCom), Nicosia, Cyprus, 2018, pp. 272-277, doi: 10.1109/CloudCom2018.2018.00060.

New terms so far

- **Height:** The height of a binary tree is the length of the longest path from the root node to a leaf node, which is also the maximum number of edges in any such path from the root node to a leaf. In other words, the height of a binary tree is a measure of the length of the longest path from the root of the tree to a leaf.

- **SHA:** Short for "Secure Hash Algorithm" developed by the National Security Agency (NSA) of the US, it is used in many applications to determine the integrity of data, to authenticate communications, and implement cryptographic tasks. There are two generations of SHA algorithms – SHA 1 (vulnerable and should no longer be used) and SHA 2 (SHA-224, SHA-256, SHA-384, SHA-512, SHA-512/224 and SHA-512/256) – and one SHA-3 algorithm. Keccak-256 is a hashing algorithm widely used in Ethereum, which is one of the variations of the SHA-3 (or Secure Hash Algorithm 3) standard.

- **Reverse-Engineered:** In the context of hashing, reverse engineering refers to the process of trying to recover or understand the input data (or original message) from its hash value computed by the hash function. It would be practically impossible to reverse-engineer SHA-256 to recover the original input data from its hash value. In short, if the hash is given, say for example - **"e167f68d6563d75bb25f3aa49c29ef612d41352dc00606de 7cbd630bb2665f51"**, it is practically impossible to obtain the original message.

2.6 Wallet, Transaction, and Block of Transactions

2.6.1 Wallet

Wallet is an application that handles all of your accounts in blockchain with ease. A wallet could serve not only as a means of storing money but also as a device, program, or service that holds the public keys of the recipient or recipient addresses that can be used to execute transactions from the wallet. The wallet will also handle transactions or, in other words, it will be able to encrypt and sign information.

Many wallets have launched in recent times but tread carefully on the one to invest in. A few of the popular wallets are listed below:

- Coinbase Wallet

- MetaMask

- TrustWallet

- Ledger Nano S Plus

Metamask is the best-known self-custodial Ethereum wallet. It has browser extensions for accessing their wallet within the browser. You also have a mobile app that you can use if you're not always using a browser. From there, we can use the wallet to interact with decentralized applications. At the time of writing this book, Metamask is only for Android/iOS. Its other extensions work on these browsers: Chrome, Firefox, Brave, Edge and Opera. Figure 2.5 shows a screenshot of Metamask in Chrome browser as an extension.

| Figure 2.5 | **Screenshot of Metamask chrome extension** |

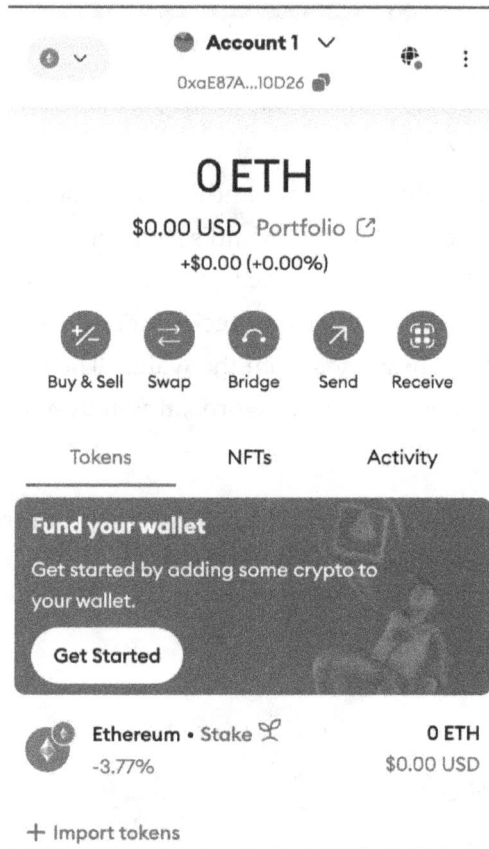

2.6.2 Transaction

Transaction is the verb or action between buyer and seller who want to communicate/agree and therefore exchange their goods, services, or asset for payment. There are three types of transactions in general i.e. finance transaction, real-estate transactions and electronic funds transaction and other types of transactions like credit transaction. A transaction is recorded with the respective bank whenever you make a purchase on your debit/credit card online. This transaction has details as to when the transaction was initiated, to whom was the money sent, the amount of transfer done, whether the money was sent to your account or whether it was debited from your account, and so on. A statement on a credit card contains all the transactions made within the past month.

Figure 2.6	A transaction made with a credit card

$52.43
Sale

📅 May 23, 2022
Transaction date

May 24, 2022
Posted date

🖥 FOSSIL #7602
LUTZ, FL 000033559

Figure 2.6 is a screenshot of a credit card transaction showing the amount, the posted date, and the transaction date along with the receiver info. This was one of the transactions on my debit card that I made when purchasing a watch from FOSSIL. Take note of the information present in the transaction. A transaction in a blockchain contains details similar to the one in Figure 2.6.

2.7 Transactions in Blockchain

In the blockchain, a transaction has a similar meaning as the one given earlier. It is a digitally signed message that is transmitted on a blockchain where funds (cryptocurrencies or fiat) are moved across in exchange for goods, assets, or services. There are a few possible types of transactions in blockchain. I mention possible since not all blockchains support the concept of smart contracts. Transactions in blockchain can be categorized as follows:

2.7.1 Regular transactions

These are transactions posted on an externally owned account managed by a human. In this case, the sender might be using the crypto exchanges or could be directly connected to the blockchain and have initiated the transaction. For example, Alice transfers 2 Bitcoins to Bob, a transaction that is purely monetary.

2.7.2 Internal transactions

Although not technically a transaction, these transactions are posted automatically from a smart contract upon fulfilling a condition and are often referred to as internal transactions. Just like how a transaction once posted to the blockchain is unalterable, similarly, a smart contract once posted to the blockchain cannot be changed. An example of internal transfer is when a user wants to exchange tokens for cryptocurrency, or when tokens are moved from one address to another (refer to Chapter 4 for more insights on tokens).

2.7.3 Contract deployment transactions

These transactions are the ones that successfully deploy the smart contract onto the blockchain. In the upcoming chapters, you will get to write a simple smart contract and have a contract deployment transaction posted onto the blockchain. An example of a valid transaction that has been posted onto the Ethereum blockchain is shown in Figure 2.7. Let's closely look at all the fields present in the transaction – Status, Block#, Timestamp,

From address, To address, Value of the transaction made, Fee charged for the transaction, and Gas price. The fields present on a transaction are blockchain-specific.

Figure 2.7	A random transaction[9] that was posted onto the Ethereum blockchain.

⑦ Transaction Hash:	0x8b93f0c99d587b9d135c34023cd4a6272a8420e73b2b89ac8c33fdf90251abbb ⓒ
⑦ Status:	✓ Success
⑦ Block:	⧖ 21098015 2 Block Confirmations
⑦ Timestamp:	⏱ 23 secs ago (Nov-02-2024 05:57:11 AM UTC) | ⏱ Confirmed within 1 sec
⚡ Transaction Action:	▸ Transfer 1.91161 ($4,798.91) ETH To 0x5F735A5cD685c61E2E9a7c48024b7b5f3Fa06a0B
⑦ Sponsored:	
⑦ From:	0x95e0b7d26dC194FEcff54ce1E2eaB31cda64b30e ⓒ
⑦ To:	0x5F735A5cD685c61E2E9a7c48024b7b5f3Fa06a0B ⓒ
⑦ Value:	◈ 1.91161 ETH ($4,798.91)
⑦ Transaction Fee:	0.000076573532511 ETH ($0.19)
⑦ Gas Price:	3.646358691 Gwei (0.000000003646358691 ETH)

Transactions, no matter the type, require a fee to be sent along with the amount being transferred in order to be posted on the blockchain. Furthermore, we can see that it is precisely these fees paid by the user that sustain the blockchain, giving miners the additional incentive to run nodes and (as we will see in the next section) to participate in the process of adding each new block of transactions. Who verifies this new block of transactions, and ensures that the original backing Bitcoins have not been faked or in any way double-spent? Here is where we get to the fun part of any blockchain – the part where miners make "trillions of trillions of attempts every second". The amount of transaction fee to be sent depends on various factors.

---

9. An Ethereum transaction from https://etherscan.io

As highlighted earlier, a transaction contains details entailing the sender, receiver, amount of funds transferred (value), gas price, gas limit, data, timestamp, and more. Along with the above-mentioned fields, a transaction also contains a hash address containing 64 hex characters which can be used to identify itself uniquely. A more detailed explanation of the attributes present in a blockchain is shared below:

- **Recipient address:** The address of the recipient, or "to" address, or output address. This is the address where the cryptocurrency will be sent to. In case the recipient is an externally owned account, the transaction transfers the value. And in case the recipient is a smart contract account, the transaction will execute the smart contract code (more about smart contracts in detail in Chapter 5).

- **Sender address:** The address of the sender, also known as the "from" address or input address of the one who initiated the transaction, essentially.

- **Digital signature:** A clear-text cryptographic signature based on the sender's private key that proves the receiver had not tampered with the message while retaining its authenticity and integrity.

- **Nonce (sometimes called a "random number"):** A randomized number that is part of the transaction sending and acts as a "Proof-of-Work" (Section 3.4 in Chapter 3 discusses this idea in detail), creating uniqueness for that specific transaction so to prevent replay attacks and/or double-spending[#].

- **Value/Amount:** The cryptocurrency transferred from sender to recipient. For Log entries in Ethereum blockchain, the cryptocurrency is "Ether" (the value is quoted in WEI# for Ethereum).

- **Transaction fee:** The amount of money/cryptocurrency a sender has to pay to motivate a potential miner responsible to include the transaction in a block and thereby confirm it on the blockchain.

- **Timestamp:** The time details revolving around the transaction creation/initiation.

- **Data:** Optional field to include any arbitrary data within the transaction. Usually, this field is used when a transaction is executing a smart contract and the user would like to store/retrieve information from the smart contract. Not all blockchains have this field in the transaction attributes; only blockchains that are smart contract-oriented will have this field visible in the transaction.

- **Gas limit:** The maximum amount of gas units that can be consumed by the transaction. Units of gas represent computational steps. The higher the computation performed by a smart contract, the higher the gas fees. Gas limit is the maximum amount of work the user is estimating a validator/miner will do on the transaction. The transactions involving smart contracts usually require more computational work and hence require more gas fees.

Caution

If you make an incorrect transaction on your bank account, chances are that the transaction could be reversed by raising a request with customer service. No such things can be done in blockchain. Make sure to double/triple-check the recipient address while sending a transaction on a blockchain. If the transaction is made to the wrong address:

- The blockchain doesn't warn you anything about an invalid address

- The transaction, if successful, cannot be reversed

- The currency will be transferred to a public address that cannot be accessed by anyone and the cryptocurrency will be sitting ducks in that public address and become unusable. That means once a transaction has been completed and money transferred, there is no third party to control the transaction via P2P.

Figure 2.8 shows transaction details from the Bitcoin blockchain. Notice that most of the fields are similar to the previous transaction shown in Figure 2.7 which is from the Ethereum blockchain.

Figure 2.8   A sample transaction in the Bitcoin blockchain

Advanced Details

Hash	03c3-88fa	Time	05 Feb 2023 01:24:37
Age	0m 35s	Inputs	1
Input Value	0.18665068 BTC	Outputs	2
	$4,278.08	Output Value	0.18660322 BTC
Fee	0.00004746 BTC		$4,276.99
	$1.09	Fee/B	21.378 sat/B
Fee/VB	33.660 sat/vByte	Size	222 Byetes
Weight	261	Weight Unit	8.460 sat/WU
Coinbase	No	Witness	Yes
RBF	No	Locktime	0
Version	2	BTC Price	$22,920.26

2.8 Mining – Get the Axe!

Recapping so far: Blockchain establishes a way for users to exchange money or other assets directly with one another, without the need for any centralized authority like banks, for example. The transactions verified, protected, and recorded on the blockchain should be doing so without any external oversight by a third party. Furthermore, blockchain's decentralized technology should permit a distributed network of miners to independently verify and record transactions on the chain.

Three different ways to obtain cryptocurrency are detailed below:

Scenario #1: Both the users have accounts in the Blockchain, and can transfer cryptocurrency by making a transaction on the blockchain.

Scenario #2: A lot of exchanges where you can buy cryptocurrency using FIAT like US Dollar, British Pound Sterling, Indian Rupees etc. Of course, there shall be a small commission for choosing this option and that is the price for getting cryptocurrency easily and faster. Kraken, Coinbase, Binance are some of the top crypto exchanges.

Scenario #3: The third and last way to obtain cryptocurrency is to work as a miner where if you manage to mine any block to the blockchain, you will be rewarded with cryptocurrency by the blockchain. This reward is usually sent directly to the public address that was used to mine in the first place.

Definition of Mining

Mining is the process by which new coin units are introduced into the circulating system. Simply put, mining means adding a transaction or transactions to a block and then adding that block to the blockchain. The method used for checking the validity of a certain transaction may differ from one blockchain to another. The architecture of how this check is done on the blockchain essentially defines the level of computational power that would be needed to mine a block into the blockchain. The method used for the validation step is determined by the consensus algorithm used in that blockchain, as detailed in Chapter 3. In the case of Bitcoin, that algorithm is Proof-Of-Work (PoW). Blockchains using Proof-of-Work consensus algorithms need exponentially more computational power compared to blockchains that don't use Proof-of-Work as the consensus algorithm.

The process of mining relies on specialized hardware called a "mining rig" as nowadays, a normal PC is not powerful enough to solve the mining problem. Mining rigs are graphics processing units (GPU) rather than central processing units (CPU) as is the case with the traditional personal computer. Some mining rigs are even equipped with multiple graphics processing units to speed up computations.

The first computer/miner to find the solution to the problem is awarded some cryptocurrency and the process repeats. The award given to the miner varies from blockchain to blockchain. Not only does the process of mining add a block to the blockchain but also generates new cryptocurrency. Mining is very important in any blockchain not just because it releases more coins into circulation, but because mining validates and secures a blockchain which is more the reason why blockchain doesn't need a third party for trust. Figure 2.9 shows a sample mining rig; notice the multiple GPUs stacked one after another, along with significant cooling systems as the GPUs generate a lot of heat during the mining operation.

Figure 2.9 **Mining rig typically used by miners which are customized for blockchain mining practices**

Fun Fact

According to Bitcoin's whitepaper, the total number of bitcoins to be produced is a constant number – 21 million bitcoins. As of March 2024, about 19.7 million bitcoins have been mined, which leaves approximately around 1.3 million bitcoins awaiting mining and distribution into the ledger. Once that limit is reached, no more bitcoins can be created. The number of bitcoins released per day varies depending on the current block reward and the rate at which new blocks are mined. On an average, approximately 900 bitcoins are released per day.

Is a node a Miner?

Not all nodes are miners, but all miners are nodes. As mentioned in the previous section, a node in a blockchain is a component that is authorized to keep a copy of the entire blockchain and serve as a communication hub for various tasks when needed. A miner is just a node that performs additional tasks. Usually, in a PoW consensus algorithm, miners are a subset of the total nodes in the blockchain network. Miners must be a full node. A miner, in general, does what a normal node is supposed to do and in addition to that, produces new blocks of transactions. The recent improvements in the blockchain infrastructure have made it possible for light nodes to operate without needing to maintain a copy of the entire blockchain.

2.9 Nodes

A node in a blockchain is a component that is authorized to keep a copy of the entire blockchain and serve as a communication hub for various tasks when needed. A node in the blockchain will have various roles and responsibilities to fill in. What kind of node and what are its obligations depend on the type of blockchain and the details of its underlying infrastructure. In the most basic terms, every blockchain node is a device that is running the software of the underlying blockchain that it is part of. When working together, those nodes form the infrastructure of a blockchain as we know it. The main task of a blockchain node is to certify the legality of every subsequent set of network transactions that follows a previous set, i.e., a block. Every blockchain node is meant to assist in finding consensus in the distributed ledger. Each node is easily identifiable by an identifier, which makes it distinguishable from any other node. A blockchain cannot have an infrastructure without a node.

For example, a machine can be configured to operate as a node within the Ethereum blockchain by installing and running the Ethereum blockchain software. You can run it front-end via a GUI (thanks to your browser), or via the command line. Several types of nodes exist, and most of them are identified either by the blockchain's architecture or by the additional features of node functionality. However, they all consistently self-organize to ensure the integrity and resilience of the blockchain network. Some of the classifications of nodes are:

- **Full nodes:** Full nodes, taking part in the entire blockchain network, download and validate every transaction and block sent throughout the network. There is no accounting of every transaction and block, and full nodes keep a complete copy of the blockchain network and take part in the Proof-of-Work process. They check transactions and blocks against the network of rules and initiate or reject every transaction and block. That way, full nodes validate transactions and blocks secures the network to maintain its decentralized state.

- **Light nodes (SPV Nodes):** A light node, more formally known as a Simple Payment Verification (SPV) node, stores only block headers and confirms that each includes proof of work. Typically, this means that light nodes require much less storage and computational power than full nodes. Specifically, they rely on full nodes for the verification of transactions and information relating to the state of the blockchain.

- **Mining nodes / Miners: Mining nodes:** located around the world – compete to add new blocks to the blockchain by solving a complex mathematical problem at hand (first come, first served). As a reward, miners get to add the new block to the ledger. Mining nodes often require specialized hardware and consume computational resources.

- **Authority nodes:** Nodes in a Delegated Proof-of-Stake (DPoS) (explained later in the book) blockchain are elected by the token holders through a voting process. The nodes, also known as block producers or validators, are authorized by the community of token holders to validate transactions and insert their validations in new blocks. The token-holder community can elect a limited number of such authority nodes to serve as the validators, usually based on the number of cryptocurrency tokens they own but sometimes on reputation.

- **Staking nodes:** In PoS blockchains, individuals can become staking nodes by staking an agreed amount of cryptocurrency, effectively locking it away as collateral. Staking nodes will typically participate in the consensus mechanism and help verify transactions and mint new blocks. The probability of being selected to mint a new block will often be proportional to how much cryptocurrency is staked. Staking nodes are usually rewarded for staking their coins, typically in the form of more cryptocurrency.

- **Seed nodes:** Seed nodes are initially configured nodes that serve as entry points for new nodes to join the network. They provide the initial list of peers to connect to, helping new nodes discover and connect with other participants in the network. They play a role in ensuring the network's growth and maintaining a robust and well-connected peer-to-peer infrastructure.

A complete node is one in which the entire contents of the blockchain are present and has the most up-to-date block history. The more the number of complete nodes in the blockchain, the more the blockchain can withstand hackers, power outages, and other malfunctions. The total number of nodes in Bitcoin is about 14,000. As Bitcoin is a public blockchain, the number of nodes and access to the blockchain is not limited, and thereby, the number of nodes is not constant. To obtain the most recent number of nodes in the Bitcoin blockchain, refer to the bitnodes.io website which has a history of the number of nodes in Bitcoin dating back seven years. A high node count ensures the resiliency of the network, which is one of the reasons why Bitcoin cannot be infiltrated by one single node.

New terms so far

- **Difficulty:** The harder it is to mine a block, the more difficult the "difficulty" is. Usually, the greater the number of blocks added to a blockchain, the harder the difficulty.

- **Wei:** The smallest unit of ether is Wei (each ether in Ethereum is 1018 wei). The smallest denomination in Bitcoin money is Satoshi, while in the core USD currency, a penny is the smallest denomination.

Unit	Wei value	Wei	Ether value
wei	1 wei	1	10^{-18} ETH
kwei	10^3 wei	1,000	10^{-15} ETH
mwei	10^6 wei	1,000,000	10^{-12} ETH
gwei	10^9 wei	1,000,000,000	10^{-9} ETH
microether	10^{12} wei	1,000,000,000,000	10^{-6} ETH
milliether	10^{15} wei	1,000,000,000,000,000	10^{-3} ETH
ether	10^{18} wei	1,000,000,000,000,000,000	1 ETH

- **Double-spending:** The double-spending problem is the issue of allowing a currency to be spent more than once. For example, Alice has $10 and has to send Bob $7 and Charlie $6. Alice will not have sufficient funds to make both transactions. This problem is, in practice, resolved for other digital transactions by banks, who process these transactions one at a time. In blockchains, the double spending problem is eliminated because of the consensus algorithm inside the blockchain.

- **Rig:** They contain multiple mining devices (CPU, GPU, FPGA, or ASIC) and additional parts such as a motherboard, power supply, cooling system, and memory, all of which work together to give a greater output power, thus increasing the odds of a reward. So, what does a mining rig do, in practical terms? It works 24/7 to earn yourself some altcoin! You could say your home would have a little money making machine.

Key-Terms

Block	Digital signature	Double-spending	Hashing
Merkle tree	Mining	Private key	Public key
SHA-256	Transactions	Wallet	

Quiz

1. The practice and study of techniques for making communication secure is called:

   a. Cryptography

   b. Artificial Intelligence

   c. Cryptocurrency

   d. Blockchain

2. What is used to verify the authenticity of transactions?

   a. Public key

   b. Digital signature

   c. Transaction

   d. Block

3. The private key is shared with other participants:

   a. True

   b. False

4. The process of converting an arbitrary length of characters into a fixed length of characters is called:

   a. Scripting

   b. Mining

   c. Marketing

   d. Hashing

5. **A hash value can be reversed to obtain the original plain text.**

   a. True

   b. False

6. **The cryptocurrency unit used in the Ethereum blockchain is:**

   a. Satoshi

   b. Wei

   c. Block

   d. XRP

7. **What is a double-spending problem?**

   a. Being able to send multiple payments

   b. Being able to send multiple payments without having sufficient funds

   c. Being able to send two payments to the same receiver

   d. None of the above

8. **A combination of multiple mining devices combined to increase the output power is called a:**

   a. Miner

   b. Computer

   c. Rig

   d. All of the above

9. **Which hashing algorithm does Ethereum use?**

   a. SHA–1

   b. SHA–2

   c. SHA–3

   d. None of the above

10. **A block in a blockchain can never have two transactions with the same nonce.**

    a. True

    b. False

Answers	1 – a	2 – b	3 – b	4 – d	5 – b
	6 – b	7 – b	8 –c	9 – c	10 – a

Chapter Summary

◆ A digital signature in blockchain is when someone signs a transaction.

◆ A block consists of one or more transactions.

◆ Merkle tree data structure is used to place the transactions inside a block.

◆ Regular, Internal, and Contract deployment transactions are different types of transactions in a blockchain.

◆ The process by which transactions are validated and added to the blockchain is called Mining.

◆ Mining rigs have a higher chance of earning a reward on blockchain as they are specifically designed to solve complex math problems.

Chapter **3**

Blockchain Types

So far, we have grazed the surface of blockchain by getting to know its fundamentals and also by introducing new terminologies in the first chapter. The second chapter dived a little more into the fundamentals and described the internals of a blockchain. Although we have looked into the structure of a blockchain, not every blockchain is the same. That doesn't mean that one blockchain is completely different from another. While the underlying architecture of each blockchain differs in some way, it should be understood that the basics remain exactly the same in every blockchain that came into existence after the Bitcoin blockchain went online in 2009. If you want to grasp the essence of blockchain, you cannot go wrong by simply acknowledging that it brings along immutability, full transparency, security, and no interference by third parties. This chapter dwells on the different types of blockchain and the different practices for mining consensus algorithms along with diving deeper into the concepts of distributed ledger.

After studying this chapter, you should be able to:

- Understand the basics revolving around the concepts of P2P

- Explain the different types of blockchain

- Differentiate between the mining/consensus algorithms used in blockchains

- Understand the problem of Byzantine generals

- Understand how mining consensus is a solution for Byzantine Generals problem

---

3.1 Peer-to-Peer (P2P)

We have often used the terms "blockchain" and "distributed ledger" interchangeably. But where does this ledger reside? Does it sit on your personal device or perhaps in an underwater tunnel? The blockchain ledger, in fact, operates as a decentralized database dispersed across a network of computers, often termed as nodes. These nodes, scattered across the network, each uphold a complete replica of the blockchain ledger.

Similarly, P2P[10] platforms connect users directly with each other, eliminating the intermediary. Consider Figure

---

10. Schollmeier, Rüdiger. (2001). A Definition of Peer-to-Peer Networking for the Classification of Peer-to-Peer Architectures and Applications. Proc. of the First International Conference on Peer-to-Peer Computing. 101 - 102. 10.1109/ P2P.2001.990434.

3.1 illustrating a P2P architecture, showcasing seamless communication among five distinct devices without external intervention. A real-life analogy for the P2P concept could be depicted as follows: imagine a gathering of you and 10 of your friends. Within this group, every individual can communicate with one another freely and everyone can see everyone at any point in time. If, for instance, you lend $10 to a friend, everyone present will be aware of this transaction. Likewise, all exchanges within the group become common knowledge.

The term P2P aligns closely with the essence of blockchain. Refining our understanding of blockchain, we can encapsulate it as a P2P network serving as a decentralized ledger for digital assets. In this context, P2P signifies a decentralized system wherein each computer maintains an identical ledger copy, validating its integrity with other nodes to ensure data accuracy. This decentralized approach underpins the blockchain's ability to maintain authenticity and trust without centralization.

Defined as a distributed network architecture, a P2P network thrives on participants sharing their hardware resources — processing power, storage capacity, network link capacity, and printers. These shared resources enable the network to provide services and content, such as file sharing or collaborative workspaces. This technology facilitates global data storage across thousands of nodes, with any node capable of accessing the blockchain entries at any time. Nodes, sometimes interchangeably termed as peers, represent equally privileged participants in the blockchain network, typically comprising computers but also encompassing devices like phones or laptops, owing to advancements in hardware and software.

A blockchain architecture integrates the principles of P2P to bypass intermediary third parties. In this setup, when a transaction occurs within the blockchain network, it is promptly recorded by every participating node. With no centralized server in a P2P system, the entirety of the blockchain ecosystem resides within nodes.

| Figure 3.1 | P2P network, where all the participants share data without central authority |

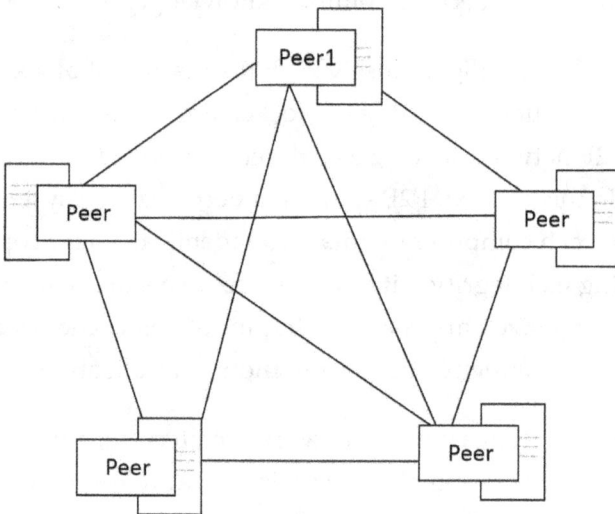

3.2 Centralized vs P2P Architectures

In the book, we have frequently emphasized that the key to a blockchain is the concept of "lack of centralization," and this section will explore the distinction between centralized and P2P (decentralized) architectures. A centralized architecture refers to a computing or organizational system in which control, decision-making, and data storage are concentrated within a single central entity or location. In a traditional newspaper publishing company, the editorial board acts as a central authority, overseeing content, layout, and distribution decisions. Editors curate stories, journalists submit work for approval, and administrative functions like advertising sales are managed centrally. This structure ensures consistency but may also limit diversity by restricting the variety of perspectives and slows down decision-making by adding multiple layers of approval and coordination that are needed for an article to be published. Figure 3.2 shows the deception of a centralized architecture. The following table differentiates both the architectures that are discussed so far.

Centralized Model	P2P Model
This architecture uses the client/server model in which one or more clients can establish a connection to the server. Responses are sent from the client and received at the server end. The responses are processed and the result is sent back to the clients.	Every node makes its own decision. The decision made by a node is then approved by all the nodes after checking the authenticity and validity of the transaction.
Single point of failure; if the server has no backup and if it fails, all the connections and the client requests will have to stop.	No such thing as a single point of failure in P2P as all nodes have the exact same copy of the blockchain as the entire network.
After a certain extent, server scaling will be limited. No matter how much increase in hardware/software is done on the server side, the cost/output ratio will not see a significant increase.	Each node can scale hardware and software independent of the network which will increase the performance of the entire system.

Centralized Model	P2P Model
Updating to a server is quick and efficient, as centralized models have fewer nodes. It requires less communication, thereby making it easier for the updates to be shipped live.	Difficult to achieve tasks that need to be performed on all the nodes, as there is no single point of command or a chain of command.
Examples: Accessing a website is a classic example of a centralized model. When you access a website, you are a client reaching out to a server to access content.	Examples: Every single blockchain architecture uses the P2P architecture. Bitcoin, Ethereum, Hyperledger, and so on.
Data can be altered and deleted on the server side. On top of that, data is private, implying that one client's details might not be visible to all the other clients.	Data is visible to every single node connected to the blockchain. Data written on the blockchain cannot be altered or deleted.
Centralization will have higher chances of data being able to be censored.	There would be cases where erasing the data is sometimes beneficial. With blockchain, censorship becomes very hard given the fact that it is not possible to alter the data once written onto the blockchain.

Figure 3.2 Centralized network, where all clients are connected to one server

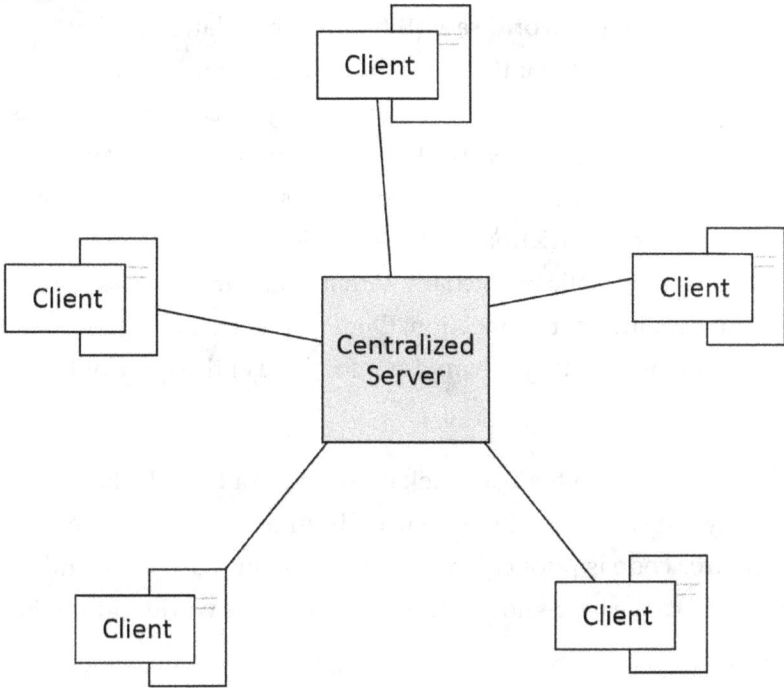

3.3 Types of Blockchain

Blockchains can be placed into various categories; however, blockchains perhaps are most commonly classified according to their architecture, where different kinds of blockchains are more suitable for different use cases. In a nutshell, there are five kinds of blockchains: Public, Private, Hybrid, Consortium and Permissioned blockchains.

3.3.1 Public blockchains

Public blockchains came first, specifically the first actual
blockchain that the world saw (Bitcoin), which later acted as
a catalyst for the rest of the blockchains that would follow.
Usually, public blockchains are run on a cryptocurrency and this
cryptocurrency is an incentive that you pay to maintain and create
the chain so that you can use hardware resources that the public
has. There is no restriction to join a public blockchain; you can
connect to the public blockchain with just any machine as long as
you have an internet connection. Once you are connected to the
blockchain as a node, you can download the entire copy of the
blockchain.

Transactions all the way back to the start of that blockchain are
publicly viewable and the code itself is an open-source code (i.e.,
the source code is publicly available) – Bitcoin, Ethereum, and
Litecoin are the best-known public blockchains worldwide right
now.

In the previous paragraphs, we have defined a public
blockchain and also described the extent to which access
is provided to the public blockchain. In the upcoming two
subsections, we will evaluate the advantages and disadvantages of
public blockchains.

Advantages of public blockchain

1. **Usability:** Anyone with an internet connection can use the
    blockchain. As long as you have an internet connection and
    a proper machine, connecting to the blockchain should be
    simple.

2. **Anonymity:** Without the nodes needing to know about each other, the transactions made through the blockchains by any of these nodes are trustable because the consensus algorithms ensure there are no fraudulent transactions. While blockchain transactions are often pseudonymous, meaning they are conducted under user addresses rather than real names, they are not completely anonymous. If the transactions are recorded using wallet addresses, then can be tracked to the origin.

3. **Transparency:** All the transactions on a public blockchain are visible to the public, thus adding more accountability.

4. **Security:** To comprise any of the data inside the blockchain, one must have control of more than 51%[11] of the computational power. Hence, the more the computational power of the blockchain, the more secure it can be. Consider a newly formed blockchain that has 10 nodes. Such a blockchain will be very insecure and prone to getting attacked by an outsider. In such cases, the blockchain can first be spread among trusted nodes. Once the computational power becomes high enough, the blockchain can then have public nodes added to it.

5. **Immutability:** The longer a transaction resides in the blockchain, the harder it is to alter the contents of the transaction. This feature can be used in applications like real estate to prove the ownership of an asset.

6. **Transfer funds:** Funds can be transferred globally from within the same blockchain without any restrictions to borders. On top of this, the fees to transfer funds are

---

11. F. A. Aponte-Novoa, A. L. S. Orozco, R. Villanueva-Polanco and P. Wightman, "The 51% Attack on Blockchains: A Mining Behavior Study," in IEEE Access, vol. 9, pp. 140549-140564, 2021, doi: 10.1109/ACCESS.2021.3119291.

considerably lower than an average financial institution like banks.

7. **Traceability:** Since the records on the blockchain are not erasable, the transactions can be easily traced, given that the blockchain creates an irreversible audit trail. This traceability of transactions comes in handy for serving as a use case in the supply chain industry. The traceability feature is a combination of immutability and transparency, which eventually benefits not only the supply chain but also the end-user by providing complete transparency of the product from the source to the destination.

Disadvantages of public blockchain

Although blockchain has created waves by introducing Bitcoin and by coming up with a new architecture that is potentially ground-breaking, public blockchains have their own disadvantages.

1. **Scalability:** The number of transactions per second in a public blockchain is much lesser compared to conventional payment systems like PayPal, VISA, and MasterCard. The number of VISA transactions alone per second is estimated to be around 25,000, while the number of transactions in blockchain per second is somewhere in the ballpark of 5-100 depending on the blockchain. The difference from 25,000 to 100 is why public blockchains haven't yet completely replaced the financial market.

2. **Deregulation:** Public blockchains are not regulated by central authorities, which makes it more difficult for users to protect their assets.

3. **Energy consumption:** As highlighted earlier, public blockchains usually run on a cryptocurrency that will help incentivize the chain and keep it up and running. The validation of transactions added to the blockchain is done through the help of consensus algorithms. There are quite a few promising consensus algorithms that have been developed over the past years. The major algorithms are discussed in detail in upcoming sections. The blockchains (for example - Bitcoin) that use Proof-of-Work consensus algorithms require a lot of energy.

4. **Immutability:** Although immutability might sound like a really good advantage, sometimes this can also prove to be disadvantageous. It becomes very hard to correct a mistake or make any necessary adjustments. For example, storing illicit or illegal content on blockchain could potentially implicate network participants in unlawful activities. Another such example would be a case where certain information stored in the blockchain over time becomes irrelevant. Due to immutability, this outdated information in the blockchain will potentially increase the storage costs. It would be efficient if older transactions were deleted, thus keeping the blockchain smaller.

5. **Legacy systems:** Blockchain is a lot harder to integrate into legacy systems. Adding blockchain to an already established and stable system is not as easy as flipping a switch. Companies trying to integrate blockchain into their system will have to do their due diligence to see if the blockchain is covering all the bases or not.

6. **Time:** Blockchain is in its early stages and it still needs time to get settled into the industry. There are still a lot of things to be standardized in the usage of blockchains.

7. **Unforgiving:** Usually when you forget the password for an online login to your bank, a new password can be requested from the site or the customer service after validating your identity. On the other hand, there is no such thing as a "Forgot my Password" button for a blockchain. A private key once lost can never be recovered. For the same reason storing the private key makes it a much riskier job.

3.3.2 Private blockchain

Private blockchains are usually much smaller than public blockchains, given the fact that a private blockchain doesn't run on any cryptocurrency. These types of blockchains will have designated miners that can execute the consensus protocol and decide the rights for mining and rewards. Private blockchains, as the name suggests, are not open to everyone, and only select applicants can view the blockchain. Access to a private blockchain is controlled and invitations are needed to join a private blockchain. Usually, these blockchains consist of nodes that have trust in each other. Ripple and Hyperledger are some of the examples of private blockchains. Chapter 5 explores in detail about creating a private blockchain using Ethereum.

Advantages of private blockchain

1. **More control to the user:** A private blockchain is not a fully decentralized application. It is a distributed ledger that operates as a closed database secured with cryptographic concepts and the organization's needs.

2. **Ease of adoption:** One of the disadvantages of public blockchains is the difficulty of integrating into the legacy systems. This can be mitigated by using private blockchains, due to its ease of creation and flexibility that it offers.

3. **Efficiency:** Private blockchains need not worry about the focus on user identities and can prioritize characteristics like efficiency and immutability.

4. **Speed of transactions:** Since there would not be any problem-solving capability like the one in the PoW consensus algorithm, transactions can be posted much faster than a public blockchain. Achieving consensus in a private blockchain is typically faster and requires fewer computational resources compared to public blockchains. This efficiency is advantageous for applications where real-time or near-real-time confirmation of transactions is essential.

Disadvantages of private blockchain

1. **Limited decentralization:** This is not much of a disadvantage, but more of a lacking feature and on top of that an understandable one. Private blockchains are not meant for everyone, implying reduced decentralization.

2. **Reduced security in comparison to public blockchains:** While validation in a public blockchain is done anonymously, the participants involved in the validation process in a private blockchain are known. Hence, private blockchains are going to be more susceptible to security breaches due to the number of validating nodes being lesser.

3. **Lack of community involvement:** Public blockchains usually have an open-source code, and benefit heavily from a diverse and active community. On the other hand, private blockchain will lack the same level of community involvement and innovation.

4. **Scalability challenges:** The speed of transactions by which they are being added to the private blockchain is faster compared to a public blockchain. But, the scalability issues will not be far off, as the number of nodes and transactions increase in the chain. Achieving consensus in a large network may become more complex, and scalability issues could impact the efficiency of the blockchain.

Table 3.1   Differences between private and public blockchain

Characteristics	Public blockchain	Private blockchain
Security	The more the decentralization, the more the security.	The security is reliant on the trusted members of the blockchain.
Transparency	The entire blockchain is visible to everyone else.	Blockchain is only visible to the members of the blockchain.
Scalability	The higher the number of users in the blockchain, the lesser the scalability as it burdens the network with more transactions	The number of users is far less than a public blockchain and hence can be scaled to higher lengths.
Power Consumption	Public blockchains, if employing PoW, have higher power consumption to agree with the mining and consensus.	Usually, private blockchains do not have PoW as their consensus algorithms which means lesser power consumption compared to its counterparts.

Characteristics	Public blockchain	Private blockchain
Examples	Bitcoin (BTC), Ethereum (ETH), Litecoin (LTC), Bitcoin Cash (BCH), Cardano (ADA), Polkadot (DOT)	Hyperledger Fabric, Corda, Quorum, Multichain, Hyperledger Sawtooth, EOSIO

3.3.3 Hybrid blockchain

A hybrid blockchain combines public and private blockchains. Since it is a public blockchain, the public nodes will be responsible for the block consensus algorithm, that is, the nodes will verify the transactions performed in the blockchain. The private part of the chain hides the data that is sensitive and gives access to only those who have permission.

Advantages of hybrid blockchain

1. **Enhanced security:** Hybrid blockchains combine the security of both types of blockchains. On a hybrid blockchain, the public network serves as a gateway to the private network segment, thus encapsulating the latter in a closed environment. While this closed environment should reduce external threats and pre-empt unauthorized logins, it will also meaningfully lower the likelihood of a 51% attack, a weakness of some public blockchains whereby one actor or group could own the majority of the network's total computing power and gain consensus on a version of the blockchain that does not reflect the actual transactions of the entire network.

2. **Anonymous communication:** In a hybrid blockchain, participants can engage in anonymous communication

within the closed network segment. Moreover, when two parties do not trust each other, such anonymity allows them to implement secure joint computations without leaking their identities. Those sequences of anonymous interactions in a blockchain enhance the confidentiality of transactions or communications between the nodes that belong to the closed network segment.

3. **Scalability:** The scalability issue of purely public blockchains can be circumvented with a hybrid blockchain. Scaling is a challenge for the purely public blockchain as it is hampered by intrinsic drawbacks related to its decentralized nature/consensus mechanism. However, hybrid blockchain can offer a scalable solution to be implemented within the private network segment for enhanced throughput, thereby making it suitable for enterprise usage. By leveraging off-chain processing or sidechains#, hybrid blockchains can handle a larger volume of transactions while maintaining performance and efficiency. This scalability advantage makes hybrid blockchains well-suited for enterprise applications and industries with high transaction throughput requirements.

4. **Customizability:** With a hybrid blockchain, members have more control over how they implement a blockchain network by designing it to meet their needs and preferences. On a hybrid blockchain, the administrators can specify which transactions are recorded privately on the closed segment of the network, and which transactions are broadcasted on the public blockchain for all to see. This means that the organization can balance transparency with privacy by making sure that regulatory requirements are met while still keeping sensitive data confidential.

Disadvantages of hybrid blockchain

1. **Limited transparency:** Hybrid blockchain provides users with better privacy by offering a private segment on top of their open blockchain. However, there is a cost for this additional privacy: each of these private segment blockchains is completely private, which means that transactions inside the private blockchain segment are not visible to all blockchain users. This would lead to a lower level of transparency when compared to a purely public blockchain. Take the example of industrial pharmaceutical supply chains where all stakeholders need to see all the information and transactions to satisfy audit, compliance, and, ultimately, trust requirements.

2. **Complexity:** Hybrid blockchains are more complex than the public and private alternatives because of their dual nature. Setting up and running a hybrid blockchain requires administrative skills to make both the public and the private segments interact smoothly. Administrators must confront the complexity of setting permissions, granting and monitoring access controls, and maintaining data integrity across the hybrid network.

3. **Regulatory changes:** Hybrid blockchains can also be regulated differently because of the private part of the blockchain not being freely available to the anonymous public on the internet. Regulatory rules for blockchain technology are still developing, and separate regulations will apply to the – sometimes competing – parts of hybrid blockchains. Complying with rules applicable to a public and a private blockchain can be quite complicated for the operator of a hybrid blockchain. It requires navigating the

regulatory uncertainty around blockchain technology and keeping up with the regulatory changes of the relevant laws and regulations. Those laws and regulations can vary based on jurisdiction, industry, type of transaction on the network, and many other factors.

Regardless of the type of blockchain that is created, all three types of blockchain have an eye on making the distributed ledger irrevocable. For instance, the Ethereum blockchain is public, but, using the source code for Ethereum one can create a Testnet blockchain, for test purposes only. The said Testnet can be accessed by adding a Free faucet for the Testnet blockchain and is available currently at - https://goerlifaucet.com/. Also, you can launch a private blockchain based on Ethereum.

Fun Fact

Hybrid blockchains aren't just about combining public and private blockchains but combining several technologies: they include hybrid blockchain projects that leverage additional emerging technologies, such as Internet of Things (IoT) devices and artificial intelligence (AI), to create truly innovative and interconnected ecosystems. These new ecosystems, leveraging the power of multiple technologies (hence "hybrid"' ecosystems) and developing novel use cases, are targeted toward specific niches and roadblocks. One of the main ones is supply chain management; another is interoperability in healthcare data; and decentralized finance, or DeFi, is another.

3.3.4 Consortium blockchain

A consortium blockchain is a consortium-led (or "permissioned") distributed ledger that's overseen by an agreed group of two or more organizations with a shared interest or mutual goal. Use cases encapsulate both use-specific functionality and privacy functionality. A consortium blockchain has permissioned access, meaning only a predefined set of participants can both read and/or write transactions in the distributed ledger system. The distributed ledger system is decentralized in that the distribution mechanism of the control is spread out among the consortium members minimizing the exposure to a sole point of failure. For this level of "permissioned" and "decentralized" trust, a proper consensus mechanism for permissioned environments – such as Practical Byzantine Fault Tolerance (PBFT) – can be used.

Advantages of consortium blockchains

1. **Efficiency:** Transactions can be executed at a higher throughput and lower latency on consortium blockchains compared with public blockchains thanks to fewer participants and a more efficient voting process.

2. **Privacy:** Consortium blockchains offer a higher level of privacy than public blockchains as access is restricted to a known set of people. This is useful for business applications where participants might want to keep data confidential.

3. **Cost reduction:** Using the same blockchain infrastructure for the operation of multiple factors of production can save maintenance, infrastructure, and operational expenses.

4. **Trust:** Consortium blockchains leverage the trust among participants, who often have pre-existing relationships or shared interests, thereby facilitating faster decision-making and cooperation.

5. **Customization:** Because the consortium has only a handful of participants, the network can typically agree on changes or enhancements to the blockchain protocol – with tweaks and customizations.

Disadvantages of consortium blockchains

1. **Centralization concerns:** More distributed than a private blockchain, but still revolving around a pre-set list of participants which poses centralization concerns.

2. **Insufficient decentralization:** If the blockchain provider is a centralized consortium, the blockchain is not fully decentralized, and the censorship-resistant nature of public blockchains may not be replicated in a similar way in consortium blockchains – crucial security and resilience can be lost.

3. **Scalability challenges:** Scalability problems might persist, mostly dependent on the consensus algorithm being used in the consortium blockchain.

4. **Governance challenges:** It's hard to develop governance among consortium members and keep it operational (that is, work to resolve conflicts) over time. Voting on changes in the protocol, upgrading security, and resolving disputes might well need to be unanimous.

5. **Entrance barriers:** A consortium blockchain can have a vetting process for joining the network, barring new entrants.

3.3.5 Permissioned Blockchain

A permissioned blockchain is a hybrid between public and private blockchains. Anybody can interact with the hybrid blockchain as long as you have permission from the maintainer of the blockchain. Anyone can join the network as long as they go through a suitable form of identity check. Some nodes are given special responsibilities that only they can perform on the network. A simple example is that only some nodes are allowed to verify the transactions on the blockchain. This way the functionalities of the blockchain are split up among the participants.

Advantages of Permissioned Blockchains

Permissioned blockchains have many advantages over their predecessors since they combine the strongest elements of public and private blockchains.

1. **Privacy and Confidentiality:** Because participants are known in a permissioned blockchain – unlike public blockchains – there is a further element of privacy as confidential business information is better protected.

2. **Scalability:** Permissioned blockchains can achieve higher transaction throughput and scalability compared to public blockchains, as they don't face the same level of computational overhead associated with consensus mechanisms involving a large number of unknown participants.

3. **Efficiency:** Because participants are known and trusted, consensus mechanisms can be more efficient. This allows for faster transaction validation and reduced energy consumption compared to PoW used in public blockchains.

4. **Governance and Compliance:** Permissioned blockchains offer more control over governance and regulatory compliance. This is necessary in areas of activity where adherence to particular, often industry-specific rules and regulations is integral.

5. **Customization:** Participants can customize the blockchain network specifications to their needs regarding consensus algorithms, data access, and smart contract functions.

6. **Performance:** As the number of participants is limited by the administrators, the performance is significantly better. On top of that, not all nodes are performing the same task, and the tasks inside the blockchain are split amongst the participants. Having the nodes that validate the transactions pre-determined will also serve as a beneficiary.

7. **Cost:** With performance comes the benefit of cost as the total cost of the network and also the cost to validate a transaction is significantly reduced compared to permissionless blockchains.

8. **More control:** Permissioned blockchains, as they have administrators and some sort of centralization in organizing the blockchain, will be more organized and the rules that need to be set up over the network can be faster. Also, the nodes on the permissioned blockchain are highly likely to work together to upgrade/update the blockchain.

Disadvantages of Permissioned blockchains

The primary drawback of a permissioned blockchain is that it inherently assumes that the participants in the blockchain will be cooperative. It might be possible for a small group of collaborators to tamper with the network's integrity.

1. **Centralization Concerns:** Some argue that permissioned blockchains may introduce centralization, as a governing authority or group of authorities often manages the permissions. This can lead to concerns about censorship and control.

2. **Reduced Decentralization:** Permissioned blockchains are inherently less decentralized than public blockchains, as the network is operated by a select group of known participants. This can affect the trustless nature of the system.

3. **Trust Requirements:** Participants need to trust the entity managing permissions. If the governing authority is compromised or acts maliciously, it can undermine the integrity of the entire network.

4. **Potential for Bias:** The process might introduce bias in participant selection, potentially excluding certain entities and limiting the inclusivity of the network.

5. **Implementation Challenges:** Developing and bringing a permissioned blockchain to life takes more planning and coordination with other participants, which can be hard, especially in very large networks with diverse stakeholders.

Differences between consortium and permissioned blockchains

The table below gives you the difference between consortium and permissioned blockchains at a glance:

Table 3.2   Differences between consortium and permissioned blockchains

Characteristics	Consortium blockchain	Permissioned blockchain
Security	Typically offers strong security as it's governed by a group of pre-selected organizations	Also provides robust security, but access control is more centralized, often managed by a single entity.
Transparency	Transparency is limited to the consortium members, with shared control over data access.	Transparency is controlled by a central authority, which decides who can view or interact with the blockchain
Scalability	Can scale efficiently as the network size is predetermined and managed by the consortium.	Can be highly scalable, with the central authority optimizing the system for performance and growth
Power Consumption	Generally more energy-efficient since it uses consensus mechanisms that require less computational power.	Also energy-efficient, often optimized for minimal power consumption due to centralized control.

Characteristics	Consortium blockchain	Permissioned blockchain
Examples	R3 (used by financial institutions), Hyperledger Fabric (used by various industries)	Ripple (used for cross-border payments), Corda (used for financial services)

New terms so far

- **Legacy system:** Legacy system refers to outdated software and/or hardware used in computing, but which remains in use. If we are talking about replacing the system with blockchain, the system that is being replaced is the legacy system. Although the legacy system continues to fulfill its original purpose, it lacks the flexibility for expansion, making a new system potentially more valuable.

- **Client/server model:** A distributed application architecture that splits up tasks or workloads between servers, who provide a resource or service, and service-requesters (or clients), who request a service by asking a server to perform a task. For example, if you wanted to open a Google website, you'd be the client, requesting your computer's server (the Google server) to display the Google page.

- **Sidechains:** Parallel blockchains running alongside the main blockchain that allow for specific on-chain transactions or smart contracts that don't need to be recorded or processed immediately on the main chain, thereby preserving its capacity while offloading non-critical transactions to sidechains, thus providing features that make it possible to process transactions faster and more efficiently and prevent congestion. Sidechains can map to the main chain and use the same consensus mechanism or use different consensus mechanisms or even have specialized features for certain use cases. Sidechains can be sterilized through two-way pegging mechanisms to avoid centralization concerns.

3.4 PoW, PoS and PBFT

So far, we have introduced the term consensus in quite a few places. The following section goes in-depth into three of the most well-known consensus algorithms — Proof-Of-Work (PoW), Proof-Of-Stake (PoS)[12] , and Practical Byzantine Fault Tolerance (PBFT). Due to the fast-paced evolution of blockchain as a technology, there have been several new and efficient consensus algorithms being developed - Delegated Proof of Stake, Proof of Elapsed time, Proof of Capacity, Proof of Burn, Proof of Activity, Proof-of-Authority, and so on…

3.4.1 PoW – Proof-of-Work

Proof-of-work* was originally introduced in the Bitcoin paper. This algorithm is the novel solution for a famous problem termed - Byzantine Generals problem. The Byzantine problem is a classic problem of distributed systems, and PoW, which is a consensus

---

12. Lin, Shijie. (2023). Proof of Work vs. Proof of Stake in Cryptocurrency. Highlights in Science, Engineering and Technology. 39. 953-961. 10.54097/hset.v39i.6683.

algorithm, addresses the Byzantine problem to ensure the immutability of peer-to-peer transactions between two unknown parties without a third-party vendor. Let's have a closer look at what a Byzantine problem is, and then understand how the solution of this problem allows us to create a decentralized and distributed system without central authority.

Byzantine Generals Problem

This is a communication problem[13] – multiple local parties can't agree on the correct solution without an arbiter they can trust. The math behind the communication problem goes back to the story of the generals. There were a couple of generals who were far apart from each other and had to attack on the same day and at the exact same time on the Byzantine Empire. Only one problem, in the 15th century, there was no social media to share status, and positions and definitely no internet, no television, no radio and there was no postal service too. So the only way that all the generals could communicate in the 15th century would be by letters delivered by private messengers.

---

13. Lamport, L., Shostak, R., & Pease, M. (1982). The Byzantine generals problem. ACM Transactions on Programming Languages and Systems (TOPLAS), 4(3), 382–401.

Self-Learning Management Series

Figure 3.3   **Every messenger is trustworthy.**

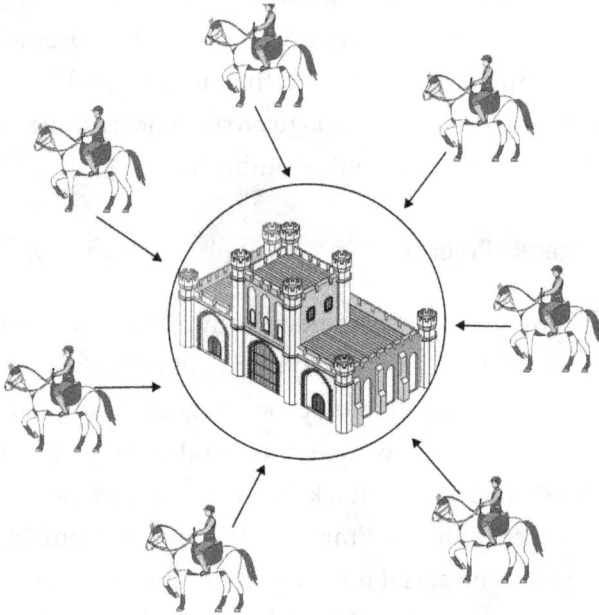

Each general would have a messenger who would communicate the time of the attack to all other generals. If all the messengers are trustworthy, then there are no issues (as shown in Figure 3.3) – All the generals will be able to land a coordinated attack on Byzantine and siege the empire. This is indicated in Figure 3.3, using the arrows pointed towards the fort, implying that all generals are marching towards the fort. VICTORY!!! In reality, that is not the case most of the time. What if one or more of the general's messengers deliberately propagates a different time for the attack to other generals (as highlighted in Figure 3.4)? Notice that in the figure, there are three untrustworthy generals (indicated by arrows pointed outwards) and four trustworthy generals (indicated by arrows pointed towards the fort). This would result in generals attacking at different times and not being able to capture Byzantine. DEFEAT!!! Not only is it a loss in the battlefield but a loss of resources too.

Scenario where there are untrusted generals

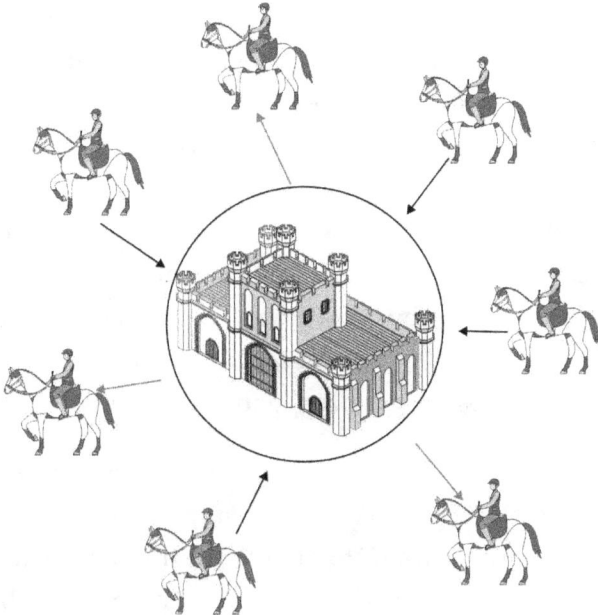

The reason we are talking about history lessons in a computer science-related textbook is that the Byzantines problem is synonymous with the problem that is posed in blockchain architecture. If there is no single consensus algorithm in the blockchain, the blockchain cannot be agreed upon. By the time anyone can tell the difference between the original one and the fake one, there will be multiple copies of blockchain on the network and it will be hard to tell which one is a trustworthy chain. The solution to the Byzantines problem is the one that is used in blockchain to prevent untrusted parties.

Solution to Byzantine Generals Problem

The solution to the Byzantine problem is that all the generals before going ahead with the attack have to agree on a time. Consider the same problem again, but this time the messengers while propagating the time, will also include the respective general's signature and timestamp of the approval. If a messenger tries to propagate a different time, it will clearly indicate that the messenger is trying to propagate the incorrect time on purpose. For the treacherous messenger to succeed, he must change the timestamps of all the other messengers who have propagated so far, which requires modifying the timestamps of the signed generals. The only way the treacherous messengers will succeed is if he has more than 51% of the messengers working with him and all of the corrupt messengers propagating at different times.

The same principle is used in blockchain; every transaction recorded in the blockchain has a timestamp attached to it. If a node in the blockchain wants to modify the transaction, it has to make the entire network agree with the said change. The bigger the network the more impossible it becomes. The older the transaction, the harder it becomes to modify, and this is possible due to the hashing algorithm used in the blockchain. PoW relies on miners racing to find the appropriate hash. All the unconfirmed transactions that are yet to be added to the blockchain are present in the Memory pool. The miners select transactions from the memory pool[#], verify the transactions, and then validate them before adding them to the blockchain. The miner who appends a block to the blockchain will be rewarded with the cryptocurrency (often referred to as virtual currencies) of the blockchain.

> **Fun Fact**
>
> Proof-of-Work was originally designed as an anti-spamming measure. Adam Back, a computer scientist, had in 1997 suggested a proof-of-work scheme called "Hashcash" wherein senders of email could include a small computational puzzle in a message: recipients would see it as a sign of legitimacy if they could solve the puzzle, which required an amount of computation. Hashcash didn't end up being used for email, but it helped to set the stage for the PoW consensus mechanism used in blockchain technology today

3.4.2 PoS – Proof-of-Stake

The majority of the recently created blockchains abandon PoW, in favor of PoS due to the limitations of PoW. Stake, aka Proof-of-Stake, is an alternative hybrid PoW consensus mechanism to validate all the transactions into the block presented, used to process a transaction in the blockchain. Stake is a concept where a coin holder becomes the participant that authenticates all the transactions, differing from PoW where miners use rigs to compete for the correct identifying hash involving computing power.

Members, known as validators, are selected, according to their weight, which equals the amount of cryptocurrency they hold and are willing to "stake", or lock up as collateral; often this is a pseudo-random algorithm that depends on the size of each participant's stake.

The validators selected to propose the next block must then validate the transactions, appending the block to the blockchain. Validators are incentivized to do this honestly since errors or malicious code will result in them losing their stake.

The main advantage of PoS is that it is capable of being more energy-efficient than PoW systems (it doesn't require miners to continually generate thousands of computing solutions to verify blocks), that it can lead to faster confirmation times and much lower fees, and that this makes PoS more scalable and usable.

On the other hand, PoS systems also have their own challenges and considerations, such as centralization or the concentration of power in the hands of richer players who control more stakes. Techniques to resolve such kinds of issues utilize a concept called staking delegation to entice less powerful validators to gather more network influence or slashing, a punishment for honest players who act maliciously.

For example, PoW is what Ethereum started with but is in the process of moving to PoS. And since Ethereum is moving to PoS, it is also set on becoming more scalable, more secure, and more sustainable. This process of Ethereum moving from PoW to PoS is referred to as the Merge. Every blockchain has its own barriers to enter as a validator, so to speak. For Ethereum, 32 ETH must be staked by a user before that user can become a validator.

3.4.3 Practical Byzantine Fault Tolerance (PBFT)

Practical Byzantine Fault Tolerances, abbreviated as PBFT[14] refers to a distributed computing system's ability to avoid the impact of fault-prone nodes. PBFT is a consensus algorithm first proposed by Miguel Castro and Barbara Liskov in 1999. It is an algorithm based on state machine replica replication, which is used to solve the problem of state machine replica consistency in distributed systems and allows the correct implementation of consensus when the fault node does not exceed the total network node $(N-1)/3$. Zilliqa is another blockchain that employs PBFT in combination with PoW-like complex computations round for every 100th block.

Characteristics

PBFT assumes that no more than one-third of the nodes in the network are faulty or malicious. It operates under the asynchronous network model, meaning that there are no bounds on the time it takes for messages to be delivered or for nodes to process messages.

Working

PBFT operates in a replicated state machine model[#] where each node maintains an identical copy of the state. The algorithm proceeds in a series of rounds, where a leader is selected for each round. The leader proposes a block of transactions to be added to the blockchain. The other nodes in the network receive the proposal and respond with a vote indicating whether they agree or disagree with the proposed block. Once a node collects enough

---

14. Miguel Castro and Barbara Liskov. 1999. Practical Byzantine fault tolerance. In Proceedings of the third symposium on Operating systems design and implementation (OSDI '99). USENIX Association, USA, 173–186

votes, it broadcasts a message to all nodes to commit the block. If a node receives enough commit messages, it adds the block to its local blockchain and informs other nodes.

Voting and Agreement

In a series of voting and communication steps, nodes vote on whether to accept the proposed block. The algorithm's clever design guarantees that even if malicious nodes join the network, honest peers can reach a consensus on the order and validity of transactions.

Fault Tolerance

PBFT is, in fact, Byzantine Fault Tolerant: which means it can guarantee safety even with malicious nodes among the participants of the consensus protocol. For this to happen, however, the number of faulty nodes must be strictly less than one-third of all the nodes.

Use Cases

PBFT has been used in numerous blockchain and distributed ledger systems to reach agreement among the nodes in a decentralized network. It has been used widely in applications where transactional trust is a key concern, such as in many financial systems and cryptocurrencies. PBFT is the basis for the consensus mechanism used by Hyperledger Fabric, a method of transaction processing that has high throughput and low latency and that works well for enterprise environments where the network participants are known and can be trusted up to a point. Chapter 6 dives deeper into working with Hyperledger and setting up the blockchain.

New terms so far

- **Sync:** Also called synchronization, implies being able to have the same data in, say, two or more places. For example, if you are told that two nodes are in sync, that means that the two nodes are holding exactly the same data, with both nodes having the most recent files.

- **Memory pool:** A memory pool, also known simply as a mempool, is a temporary data storage area in a blockchain protocol that holds valid as-of-now unconfirmed transactions waiting to be included in a block and added to the blockchain. If I send a Bitcoin to you, the transaction is broadcast from my wallet to the network and is entered into the mempool of every participating node (computer) that maintains the blockchain that the protocol is running on. Miners review transactions from the mempools and pick and choose which to include in the block that they'll be attempting to mine next. They do this depending upon a combination of factors, such as the size of the transaction, the fees associated with the transaction, and the network congestion taking place.

- **Open-source:** Open-source software is a software code that anybody can look at, tweak, and alter. Since the Ethereum blockchain is open-source, many newer blockchains that have been developed are essentially newer iterations of Ethereum.

- **State Machine model:** A replicated state machine model is a fancy way of saying that the entire network keeps an exact copy of the system's current status or state. When a change or an update happens, every node updates its copy in the same way, ensuring that all nodes stay in sync and agree on the state of the system at all times and thereby making sure the network functions correctly and securely, even if some nodes fail or act maliciously.

Key-Terms

Byzantine's problem	Centralized	Consensus	Consortium blockchain
Decentralized	Hybrid blockchain	P2P	Peer
Private blockchain	Proof–of-stake	Proof-of-work	Public blockchain

Quiz

1. The term used to describe the individuals or entities that create blocks in a blockchain that use the Proof-of-Work consensus algorithm is:

   a. Miners

   b. Validators

   c. Creators

   d. None of the above

2. The term used to describe the individuals or entities that create blocks in a blockchain that use the Proof-of-Stake consensus algorithm is:

   a. Miners

   b. Validators

   c. Creators

   d. None of the above

3. The memory pool holds _____ transactions

   a. unconfirmed

   b. confirmed

   c. late

   d. transactions with a high price

4. **The currency state of the blockchain holds _____ transactions.**

    a. confirmed

    b. unconfirmed

    c. late

    d. transactions only on smart contracts.

5. **The process of mining is often referred to as:**

    a. Proof-of-Stake

    b. Proof-of-Validity

    c. Proof-of-Work

    d. Proof-of-Miner

6. **What does P2P stand for?**

    a. Peer-to-Peer

    b. Password-to-Password

    c. Participant-to-Participant

    d. Private-to-Public

7. **Proof-of-Work uses high computational power.**

    a. True

    b. False

8. **Which of the following are distributed ledgers?**

   a. Bitcoin

   b. Ethereum

   c. Hyper ledger

   d. Ripple

   e. All of the above

9. **What do the miners race to get in a Proof-of-Work consensus?**

   a. Find the appropriate hash

   b. Find the correct transaction

   c. Get the cryptocurrency

   d. None of the above

10. **Which of the following can be best used to describe Proof-of-Stake?**

   a. Password

   b. Verification protocol

   c. Public key hash

   d. Transaction

Answers	1 – a	2 – b	3 – a	4 – a	5 – c
	6 – a	7 – a	8 – e	9 – a	10 – b

Chapter Summary

◆ The architecture that blockchain uses to communicate nodes amongst each other is P2P.

◆ Blockchain can be primarily classified into five different types - Public, Private, Consortium, Hybrid, and Permissioned.

◆ Each blockchain type comes with its own advantages and disadvantages.

◆ The PoW consensus algorithm is fundamentally based on the solution to the Byzantine Generals problem.

◆ Proof-of-Work, Proof-of-Stake, and Practical Byzantine Fault Tolerance are some of the prevalent consensus algorithms.

◆ PoW relies on high computational power for mining operations.

◆ PoS relies on participants' cryptocurrency ownership for block validation.

Chapter 4

Cryptocurrency

The first half of this book explored what a blockchain is, its history, and the different varieties of blockchains. In this chapter, we turn our attention to the language used around cryptocurrency, discuss the differences between digital money and fiat currency, illustrate how to transfer simple cryptocurrency from one person to another via their digital wallets and examine the difference between a cryptocurrency and a token.

After studying this chapter, you will be able to:

- Understand the basic definition of cryptocurrency
- Distinguish between fiat and cryptocurrency
- Understand the basic types of cryptocurrencies and tokens
- Distinguish between token and cryptocurrency
- Describe how to send and receive cryptocurrency
- List the most popular cryptocurrencies in the market right now

4.1 What is Cryptocurrency

Cryptocurrency, also known as crypto, is a set of digital assets that are constructed using various cryptographic techniques residing on the blockchain. This essentially enables the users of the blockchain to transfer funds without the need for a third party. In other words, cryptocurrency is a P2P system that runs on top of blockchain and allows you to send/receive payments from anyone and anywhere. As of early 2023, there are more than 1,000 cryptocurrencies in the market. The cryptocurrencies are of various kinds, some world-renowned are Bitcoin, Ethereum, and so on, and some others are pegged cryptocurrencies like Tether and Binance.

Fiat currencies, in contrast, are currencies issued by the state. Cryptocurrencies are not backed by a government; rather, they depend upon the decentralized structure of blockchain technology itself. This decentralized structure is the very one that makes cryptocurrency possible – existing outside of government and central authorities. There's so much more to know about blockchain because it's a new technology, but we know that at least cryptocurrency has the potential to impact both finance and law.

All public blockchains have a cryptocurrency, which is given as an incentive to the miner who has mined a block of the blockchain. In reality, all cryptocurrencies are kept in wallets that are maintained by the exchanges. Thus, all incentives given by cryptocurrencies are what keep the miners connected to the blockchain. A private blockchain doesn't have a cryptocurrency because a private blockchain has only trusted parties connected to it. This should explain why there are no validations needed in a private blockchain, which is why there can be no mining of blockchain and hence, no cryptocurrencies.

4.1.1 Advantages of cryptocurrency

- **Decentralization:** As cryptocurrencies are coded into a distributed computer network and do not originate from or rely on any centralized server, this gives them the potential to be more transparent, impossible to hack, and less susceptible to government or corporate censorship.

- **Transferability:** It can take days for fiat money to move around the world but cryptocurrency can move in as fast as a few minutes, depending on which blockchain you're using. Such global transfers allow access to banking in those places without much traditional banking infrastructure.

- **Security:** Cryptocurrencies use cryptographic techniques to secure transactions and verify the transfer of assets, making them impervious to fraud, hacking, and other identity theft.

- **Lower transaction fees:** Transferring cryptocurrency from person A to person B costs very little, compared with the same amount transferred by fiat currency. The premise is that there is no third party in cryptocurrency.

- **Cryptocurrency expansion:** The rising adoption of blockchain technology in use cases that go beyond the standard monetary use (such as smart contracts) provides cryptocurrencies with a crucial advantage through higher utility and industry adoption.

4.1.2 Disadvantages of cryptocurrency

- **Environmental concerns:** To generate cryptocurrency a block has to be mined blockchain (those employ PoW). Back when Bitcoin just started, it was said that mining could be done on a regular desktop/laptop. But nowadays, to mine a block into the blockchain for the Bitcoin network, a special mining rig is required. This mining rig requires very high energy consumption. Most of the mining activities in blockchain that use PoW as the consensus algorithm require high energy consumption.

- **Illegal activities:** The level of anonymity or pseudonymity in cryptocurrency transactions depends on the specific cryptocurrency and users' privacy measures. While transactions are traceable on the blockchain, users can enhance their privacy with methods like privacy coins or mixing services, making it harder to trace transactions. However, this anonymity can also enable criminal and illicit activities, as transactions used in such situations may not be easily traceable, incentivizing the misuse of blockchain for illegal purposes.

- **Volatility:** The price of the cryptocurrency is highly volatile. For example, Bitcoin's price has reached $68000 in and around November of 2021. As of October 2022, the price of Bitcoin fell back to $20000. Such high price volatility of cryptocurrency implies a higher risk in the investments of cryptocurrency.

- **Security risks:** Cryptocurrencies are 100% safe as long as the private key is not stolen. But the wallets that store cryptocurrency are a potential hacking target and there have been cases of wallets getting hacked.

- **Lost and found:** There is a possibility of losing your virtual wallet or your private key. Once lost, there is no way to regain the lost account. All the cryptocurrency attached to a lost account can never be recovered.

4.1.3 How does it compare to Fiat?

The paper currency we use right now is also called fiat currency and is used to buy/sell/trade. Even though cryptocurrency can be used as a means of payment in certain businesses (very few at the moment), not all businesses have adopted the concept of crypto and most of the businesses still use fiat currency. The disadvantages listed above are the reasons why cryptocurrency hasn't crawled its way into every business that has financial transactions involved in it. It will take a lot of time for crypto to get standardized and be used as a payment service throughout the globe. The government has to intervene in some way to standardize the cryptocurrency, while at the same time having most of the distributed features intact. The good and bad of the cryptocurrencies are still being looked into.

Fun Fact

The Song Dynasty in China was the first to issue paper money, jiaozi, around the 10th century CE. Although the notes were valued at a certain exchange rate for gold, silver, or silk, conversion was never allowed in practice.

4.2 Differences between Fiat and Crypto

Fiat	Cryptocurrency
A government-issued currency that isn't backed by a physical commodity such as gold/silver	Digital currency that runs on a decentralized network like blockchain
Has a stable value, and volatility depends on the factors revolving around a country like economic fundamentals, interest rate differentials, and political instability.	Highly volatile and the price cannot be predicted, which makes investments in crypto a high-risk investment.
United States Dollar – USD Indian Rupees – INR South Korean Won - KRW	Bitcoin (BTC) Ethereum (ETH) Ripple (XRP) Litecoin (LTC)
Foreign Exchanges exist, and they act as an intermediary to help you exchange one type of fiat currency for another.	Crypto exchanges do exist and act as a middleman between the buyer and seller of cryptocurrencies.
Fiat currency transactions are more likely to leak and be less anonymous, as financial institutions and governments keep records to ensure compliance with regulations.	It is true that cryptocurrency transactions potentially promise more anonymity; public blockchains record transactions to every participant's address. But transactional pseudonymity notwithstanding, they are broadcasted to every participant on the public blockchain and can be traced back to each "input" on the blockchain – meaning that, if your first bitcoin came from

Fiat	Cryptocurrency
	a legitimate source, a regulator could backtrack it to its origins in the blockchain.
Transactions involving fiat money have intermediaries (banks or payment processors) involved that often lead to longer processing times and higher costs of transferring funds, especially internationally.	Cryptocurrencies can be quicker and less expensive, especially across borders, which can save on high fees and dragnet monitoring.
Fiat currencies, meanwhile, are susceptible to various economic pressures (at the whim of a central bank inclined to expand the money supply, for example). As a result, the purchasing power of cash can decrease over time.	Most cryptos also have their supply fixed or capped at some level, creating an "insurable" quantity of coins that can never be exceeded. A fixed supply is one way of guarding against risks to the currency from inflationary pressures, but, at a minimum, it creates deflationary risks.
Fiat currency comes in the form of banknotes and coins, but also digital models maintained through banks and other financial institutions	These assets exist only in digital form and are stored on networks that use cryptography to ensure their security (hence the "cryptocurrency" label).

4.3 Bitcoin, Altcoins, and Fiat Money

As was discussed earlier, Bitcoin is the first cryptocurrency, and all other cryptocurrencies created after Bitcoin was often called Altcoins. In the decade after the introduction of Bitcoin, at least 100,000 altcoins have been created. Each Altcoin is supposed to have a specific purpose and a design that suits that purpose. The dynamics are similar to Bitcoin as far as how volatile its prices can be. The first altcoin created is Litecoin, which is a crypto that presumably uses a consensus algorithm that is less energy-intensive compared with Bitcoin. The most popular altcoin is Ether which is a crypto used to run the Ethereum blockchain. The market cap of the Ethereum token as of October 2022 is more than $165 billion.

4.4 Popular Cryptocurrencies Right Now

Top among the list of cryptocurrencies are Ethereum (ETH), Ripple (XRP), DogeCoin (DOGE), Solano (SOL), and many more. Every cryptocurrency uses a different architecture from the other and most of the blockchains are forked versions of the Ethereum blockchain.

The top 10 cryptocurrencies in the world as of March 2023 are as listed in finance.yahoo.com:

Symbol	Company Name	Last Price (US Dollars)	Volume	Market Cap
BTC-USD	Bitcoin USD	27176.617	16.94B	525.32B
ETH-USD	Ethereum USD	1724.1914	7.67B	211.00B

Symbol	Company Name	Last Price (US Dollars)	Volume	Market Cap
USDT-USD	Tether USD	1.0003879	26.79B	79.21B
BNB-USD	BNB USD	314.33536	534.27M	49.63B
USDC-USD	USD Coin USD	0.9997154	3.99B	33.73B
XRP-USD	XRP USD	0.46347207	2.26B	23.82B
ADA-USD	Cardano USD	0.34489134	287.66M	11.98B
DOGE-USD	Dogecoin USD	0.072968856	421.98M	9.68B
MATIC-USD	-	1.0543686	352.52M	9.57B
BUSD-USD	Binance USD USD	0.99903303	3.20B	8.02B

4.5 Tokens

A token is a digital asset or unit of value that is produced, issued, and managed on a blockchain network. Tokenization is the process of defining a token and establishing its attributes, rights, and behavior through smart contracts. As opposed to cryptocurrencies like Bitcoin and Ethereum, which have a native blockchain network where they run, a token operates on a shared, application-specific blockchain. Online crypto communities, markets, and exchanges use them as tokens of participation and rewards. Ethereum uses "ether" as a token (which is also used to pay transaction fees). There are several types of tokens, including security tokens to represent an ownership interest in a real-world asset; utility tokens which are used to access a product or service within an ecosystem; and increasingly so-called non-fungible tokens (NFTs) which represent unique, non-reproducible digital assets such as digital art or collectibles. Smart contracts code the issuance, holding, and transfer of tokens, and guarantee the security, transparency, and immutability of transactions. Tokens have applications in decentralized finance (DeFi) platforms, digital identity architectures, and decentralized autonomous organizations (DAOs), amongst many other use cases, and are crucial to further building and innovating in the blockchain space.

4.5.1 Types of tokens

Utility tokens

Utility tokens are digital assets that project issues to allow consumers to purchase goods, services, or functionalities on their platforms. They are created by projects during their initial coin offerings (called ICOs – see explanation at the end of Chapter 5) and are not meant as investments but as a "utility" currency. Various popular utility tokens include Binance Coin (BNB) – which you can use to pay transaction fees and access additional services on the Binance exchange – Chainlink (LINK), and Uniswap (UNI).

Security tokens

Security tokens reflect ownership of tangible assets, such as equity in a company, debt instruments, or ownership of real estate. As securities that adhere to existing securities laws, they provide the rights and dividends to the buyer and act as a hinge between the existing financial market and the blockchain itself to enable fractional ownership and additional liquidity.

Non-fungible tokens (NFTs)

Non-fungible tokens* (NFTs) are cryptographic digital assets that represent digital or physical items such as artworks, collectibles, rings, virtual real estate, and virtual assets (e.g., in-game items). They differ from cryptocurrencies such as Bitcoin and Ethereum, which are examples of fungible tokens because NFTs are unique and stand apart from other tokens created on the relevant blockchain. Cryptocurrencies, on the other hand, are all identical values and are interchangeable with one another, meaning that each unit of value (e.g., 1 Bitcoin, 1 Ethereum) is divisible into smaller units. An NFT, by contrast, is indivisible. Owners or creators of digital assets such as NFTs can create a record of their ownership or its authentication by linking metadata about the asset to a block on the blockchain An example of an NFT is CryptoKitties, a game created for users on the Ethereum blockchain, where you can buy, sell or breed unique digital cats that have different colors and attributes. Another example is LAND, the central asset behind the Decentraland platform, a blockchain-based virtual world. It works in a similar way to CryptoKitties, where you can buy LAND, which represents a specific area or parcel of virtual estate in that world, and then build virtual reality space on it as your avatar traverses the landscape.

Governance tokens

Governance tokens like Compound's COMP and MakerDAO's MKR are used to govern decentralized protocols and platforms by allowing holders to take part in votes that help decide everything from changes to the protocol to voting on proposals and how parameters of a network are set. This can include decisions made by groups of individuals to manage lending protocols and issue stablecoins.

Asset-backed tokens

Asset-backed tokens (such as TAURI, tAU$, or PAX Gold) represent fractional ownership of a tangible asset, such as gold, real estate, or any other actual asset. These tokens are beloved by investors because of their ability to give them a "slice" of a tangible asset. They are also frequently used to allow for the tokenization of real-world assets, making them easier to trade and transfer on a blockchain network.

Interoperability tokens

Interoperability tokens help in communications and value transfer between blockchain networks. They enable cross-chain interoperability, meaning an application built on one blockchain can interact with an application built on another blockchain. Examples include Polkadot (DOT) and Cosmos (ATOM), which connect multiple blockchains to allow for the transfer of assets and data across networks.

Fun Fact

NFTs reached their high point in 2021 when their total sales volume topped $10 billion as the market bubbled along on the back of a series of headline-grabbing auctions and celebrity musings, but the turning point for the market came in late 2021 and into 2022 when trading activity slipped and prices fell, causing many to wonder what brought on the correction and how long it would last. It would appear that, despite the reversal, there is still demand for tokenized assets and we have only begun to understand the dynamics of blockchain-based economies.

4.6 Types of Cryptocurrencies

It's been a long time since Bitcoin appeared in 2009. Since then, a myriad of cryptocurrencies have appeared, some based on the same original concept (a shared digital dataset), some not. Just as many technological innovations have happened, the original blockchain beyond Bitcoin has been undergoing improvements, proliferation, and diversification. This might be a good time to offer a slightly more detailed catalog of cryptocurrencies. There are various classifications, based on general technological features or aims.

4.6.1 Currency coins

This is one of the first types of coins out there and the most well-known category of all. Starting with Bitcoin (BTC) as an example, others include Litecoin (LTC), Bitcoin Cash (BCH), Dash (DASH), and Monero (XMR). These cryptocurrencies aim to improve Bitcoin by offering faster transaction speeds, lower costs, or enhanced anonymity.

4.6.2 Platform coins

A platform cryptocurrency supports decentralized applications or "DApps" as well as self-executing smart contracts that don't need third parties, such as lawyers or judges, to make a transaction binding.

Ethereum (ETH) is currently the leader (its tokens are the "coin of the platform") and good for developing smart contracts and DApps. Other examples of platform coins are EOS, Cardano

(ADA), and Tron (TRX). Each of these services has its own characteristics with additional benefits beyond just the token itself.

4.6.3 Privacy coins

Privacy-focused cryptocurrencies can be understood as "crypto coins with a twist" that put a premium on anonymity and privacy. Most cryptocurrencies can theoretically be identified by government authorities given access to the proper records. By contrast, privacy coins use a variety of different cryptographic techniques to hide certain elements of transactions. Instead of drawing attention to themselves, blockchain participants can perform anonymous transactions if they so desire. The most well-known privacy coins include Monero (XMR), Zcash (ZEC), and Dash (DASH), but there are many others available to choose from. While the details of each privacy coin's methods differ, all three services transmit information to the blockchain using one or more: ring signatures#, zk-SNARKs#, and coin mixing#.

4.6.4 Stablecoins

Stablecoins are cryptocurrencies that attempt to mitigate volatility in price by pegging to a stable asset (dollar, euro, gold, etc). The best-known examples are Tether (USDT), USD Coin (USDC), and Dai (DAI). Stablecoins are widely held and traded as a medium of exchange and a store of value within the crypto arena.

4.6.5 Micropayment cryptocurrencies

Micropayment cryptocurrencies focus on small-value transactions. Their strong points are the fast transfer of value, low cost of transactions, and lack of fees that are suitable for microtransactions, monetization of online content, and pay-per-use services. Nano (NANO) and IOTA (MIOTA) are DOGE competitors in the (fast) micropayment space, with fee-less or virtually free transactions per se, and hence suitable for micropayments and IoT applications.

4.7 Send and Receive

Using exchanges, fiat currency can be traded for cryptocurrency. Most of the exchanges also offer trading one cryptocurrency for another. Some of the popular exchanges in the current market are Binance, Coinbase, Robinhood, and Kraken. As the exchanges provide support, third-party fees are charged for using the services. Depending on the exchange, the fees vary. Coinbase for example, charges a flat 1% transaction fee on all cryptocurrency transactions. Sending and receiving crypto will involve having to give access to the private key to the exchanges. To send crypto, the receiver's public address is sufficient and no other information about the receiver is required. There are various ways to send and receive crypto using only Coinbase itself. One can use the mobile wallet of Coinbase or log in to the wallet on your browser and this will show many other options available to the user. Users can buy, send, receive, scan, or access other similar options as shown in Figure 4.1, which also depicts how the home page is seen as of June 2023 on the Coinbase mobile application. The same principle would apply when one wants to purchase tokens in the blockchain.

| Figure 4.1 | Coinbase mobile wallet homepage |

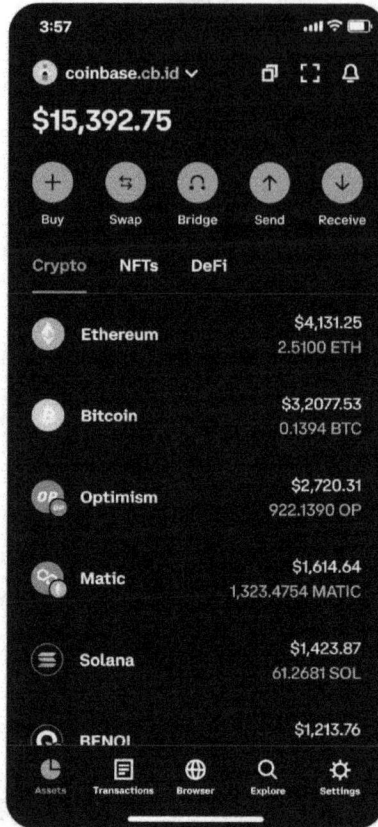

Caution

Double-check and triple-check the addresses that the cryptocurrency is being sent to. Cryptocurrencies that are sent to the wrong public address cannot be reverted. If sending large amounts, try sending the receiver as short an amount as possible. Once the receiver has confirmed the payment, you can send the actual amount

New terms so far

- **Fiat:** The term fiat is derived from Latin which means "it shall be"; or "let it be done". Fiat money has value only because the nation-state makes it so.

- **Wallet:** You use your crypto wallet to give orders to it, to sign a transaction on the blockchain; it stores your private keys in one place. A crypto wallet can be a piece of hardware or a software application.

- **Exchange:** A business that allows users to trade fiat currency for any cryptocurrencies that the exchange supports. In October 2022, Binance, the world's largest exchange, claimed to offer more than 600 cryptocurrencies.

- **DApps:** DApps, short for decentralized or distributed applications, is a program that depends on software run on a decentralized network instead of running on a single server of a centralized application. Instead of that app being hosted by a single company, the network is instead run on a blockchain, where nobody is in control of the whole network. There are many advantages to using a DApp when compared with an old-fashioned app, such as greater security, full transparency, and impossible censorship. The typical DApps will employ smart contracts for fairly complicated pre-programmed actions. Examples of Dapps include Decentralized finance (Defi), decentralized exchanges (DEXs), and GameFi (Blockchain-based games).

- **Ring Signatures:** Another approach to enhancing privacy is the usage of ring signatures. This is a type of signature that mixes in a transaction by the spender of the transaction with other transactions. Therefore, when examining the transactions on the blockchain, it looks as though there have been many potential signers of the transaction, making it difficult to tell who is sending the money. Ring signatures can be better understood with a real-life example. Suppose you and some colleagues intend to send an anonymous suggestion to managers in your large company – maybe you want to alert them to a dangerous production defect – and you want to sign the suggestion but have it appear as if your colleagues signed it too, to prove that the suggestion is legitimate. The ring signature function would let you sign it with your digital signature but mix it with the signatures of your colleagues so that, when the managers receive the message, they will know that the suggestion came from one of you, but cannot tell which one signed it. Your identity is still private, but the signature attests that the suggestion came from someone in the legitimate group.

- **zk-SNARKs:** Zero-Knowledge Succinct Non-Interactive Arguments of Knowledge (zk-SNARKs), for short, are cryptographic proofs that enable one party to prove to another party that they know something without revealing what they know. In the context of cryptocurrencies, zk-SNARKs allow for privacy as transactions can be accepted while remaining hidden from the public, such that receivers do not see the sender of the money, senders do not see the receivers of the money, and neither see the transaction amount.

- **Coin mixing:** Coin mixing ("coin tumbling" or "coin laundering") disrupts cryptocurrency's public, traceable record by mixing a user's coins with those of other users. In doing so, the provenance of the funds is obscured. The experience is likened to wadding up a dollar bill and throwing it into the air. Good luck figuring out where it came from, and where it will end up.

- **Fork:** When all the parties that are connected to the blockchain are not in agreement, alternate chains may emerge. Forks can be accidental or intentional. Intentional forks are again classified as hard forks and soft forks

Key-Terms

Altcoins	Cryptocurrency	DogeCoin	Fiat
NFT	Platform Coins	Privacy coins	Ripple
Send/Receive crypto	Solidity	Solano	Stablecoins
Tokens	Utility tokens		

Quiz

1. Which of the following currencies are highly volatile?

   a. USD

   b. Bitcoin

   c. GBP

   d. Ethereum

   e. INR

2. Fiat currencies are physical assets, and you can store one in your wallet/purse. Unlike fiat, cryptocurrencies are digital currencies, but where are they typically kept?

   a. Blockchain

   b. Exchanges

   c. Private keys

   d. None of the above

3. A stable currency maintains a relatively consistent value over time with minimal fluctuations. Which of the following currencies are stable? Select all that apply.

   a. USD

   b. Bitcoin

   c. Ethereum

   d. INR

4. **All the cryptocurrencies generated after Bitcoin are termed altcoins.**

    a. True

    b. False

5. **What is a crypto wallet?**

    a. A place to store private keys

    b. A place that stores cryptocurrency

    c. Used for making a transaction

    d. All of the above

6. **The energy required to generate cryptocurrency is:**

    a. high

    b. low

    c. dependent on a consensus algorithm

    d. cannot be determined

7. **Litecoin is advantageous to Bitcoin in this aspect.**

    a. It uses less energy to generate crypto.

    b. It uses high energy to generate crypto.

    c. It has higher volatility.

    d. Litecoin is not a blockchain.

8. **What is the primary incentive for miners in a public blockchain?**

    a. Government rewards

    b. Cryptocurrency

    c. Bank transfers

    d. Hardware components

9. **Why is it suggested that cryptocurrency adoption may take time to become standardized?**

    a. Lack of use cases

    b. High government intervention

    c. The need for standardized wallets

    d. The government's role in standardization

10. **When all the parties and the blockchain do not agree, the following may emerge:**

    a. Alternate chains

    b. New cryptocurrencies

    c. Modified wallets

    d. None of the above

Answers	1 – b, d	2 – a	3 – a, d	4 – a	5 – d
	6 – c	7 – a	8 –b	9 – d	10 – a

Chapter Summary

◆ Cryptocurrency, sometimes referred to as crypto, is a set of digital assets created using various cryptographic techniques residing on blockchain that enables the users to transfer funds across without the need for a third party.

◆ The paper currency that we have right now is also called fiat currency and is used to buy/sell/trade.

◆ Cryptocurrency payments, unlike fiat currencies, exist purely as digital entries to an online database describing specific transactions.

◆ The cryptocurrencies that are created after Bitcoin are often referred to as Altcoins (short for alternate coins).

◆ A token is a digital asset or unit of value that is produced, issued, and managed on a blockchain network.

◆ Currency, platform, privacy, and stablecoins are some of the different types of cryptocurrency coins.

This page is intentionally left blank

Chapter **5**

Potentials of Blockchain

In the four preceding chapters, we covered the basics of blockchain in general and the various types of blockchains, their characteristics, benefits, and flaws. This chapter covers the potential of the blockchain concept and will familiarize you with the knowledge required to create an Ethereum-based private blockchain. By the end of this chapter, you will know how smart contracts work, and how to create a basic smart contract and post transactions to it. We won't delve into the meticulous documentation of smart contract creation because it requires more knowledge than is provided in this book. We will, however, introduce its fundamentals by focusing on the creation of an Ethereum-based private blockchain

After studying this chapter, you will be able to:

- Understand the process for the creation of blockchain

- Create a private blockchain for testing purposes

- Send cryptocurrency over the blockchain in a private network

- Create a smart contract and post a transaction through the smart contract

5.1 Using the blockchain

As mentioned in the previous chapters, blockchain is being leveraged in various technologies – healthcare, music, realtor, security – other than just cryptocurrencies. This book will not be able to cover all the use cases of blockchain, given how broad they are in the first place. Some of the use cases will be provided as examples later on. As we know, blockchain was originally meant to be a platform for transferring money between two parties directly, without any intervention of a third party. However, after the introduction of the concepts of smart contracts in blockchain, it has gained a higher popularity and has led to different use cases within this architecture. This chapter will introduce how to create a simple yet fully functioning blockchain.

For testing, we will utilize third-party software to establish a simple blockchain. Numerous software options are available for setting up a private blockchain, with Ganache being one of the most widely employed choices along with remix.ethereum.org. Typically, Ganache is used alongside another third-party software called Truffle. By employing Ganache and Truffle in tandem, we can construct a fully operational blockchain and write statically-typed[#] smart contracts. This platform will facilitate our exploration of digital currency transactions and smart contract development.

No programming knowledge is required for Ganache and Truffle as they are third-party software that allows us to quickly fire up a personal Ethereum blockchain which you can use to run tests, execute commands, and inspect state while controlling how the chain operates. More information about the software can be found here - https://trufflesuite.com/docs/ and https://trufflesuite.com/ganache/.

5.2 Ganache

Ganache is a personal blockchain for rapid Ethereum and Corda[#] distributed application development. Ganache will function for you the whole time you are developing your dApps: you can develop, deploy, and test your dApps in a reliable and predictable environment. Decentralized applications – or dApps, or dapps – are applications that run on a blockchain network of computers, rather than one computer. DApps are thus, outside the purview and control of a single authority. Because dApps are decentralized, they are free from the control and interference of a single authority which is synonymous with the working of a blockchain.

Ganache comes in two flavors: a GUI[#] and a CLI (Both these are offered for various operating systems[15]). Ganache UI is a desktop application supporting both Ethereum and Corda technology. A screenshot of the Ganache UI is shown further into the chapter. Both the UI and CLI can be used to deploy private blockchains similar to Ethereum. According to the documentation provided

---

15. https://github.com/trufflesuite/ganache-ui/releases

on the official Ganache website, both the UI and CLI offer the
following:

- console.log in Solidity

- Zero-config Mainnet[#] and testnet[#] forking

- Forking any Ethereum network without waiting to sync

- Ethereum JSON-RPC support

- Snapshot/revert stat

- Mining blocks instantly, on-demand, or at an interval

- Impersonating any account (no private keys required!)

- Listens for JSON-RPC 2.0 requests over HTTP/WebSockets

- Programmatic use in Node.js

- Pending transactions

The Ganache application is available for 3 operating systems
- Windows, MacOS, and Linux. The installation instructions
for Ganache UI and CLI can be found here - https://trufflesuite.
com/docs/ganache/quickstart/. Once the appropriate version of
Ganache is downloaded based on your operating system, open the
application by double-clicking and going through the installation
steps. The installation steps should be very straightforward.
After opening the downloaded version of Ganache, you will be
provided with two options: "Quick Start" and "New Workspace".
To begin with, start by clicking on QuickStart. A similar screen
should appear as the one shown in Figure 5.1. Note that the
addresses shown in the figure and the addresses on your version
of Ganache will be completely different. These addresses are 10
different public accounts that we can use for testing purposes. Of
course, we can add more accounts to the blockchain as needed.

The addition of more Ethereum accounts and the functions provided by the Ganache application are discussed in the upcoming sections.

Ganache creates a test Ethereum-based network which will help us in understanding and testing all the basic functionalities of a blockchain. Some of the most common ones are transferring cryptocurrency from one account to another, writing a smart contract, deploying a smart contract, and so on.... Many professional teams use software like Ganache which helps as a testing mechanism before they deploy the smart contracts using digital currency onto Ethereum. Smart contracts deployed onto the public blockchain will have to be error-free, as there have been many known vulnerabilities through poorly written smart contracts.

Notice the different tabs present in the Ganache application:

1. The first tab, which is the one shown in the picture, gives us the complete list of accounts present in the created blockchain.

2. The second tab named "blocks" shows the total number of blocks mined into the blockchain so far.

3. On a similar note, the third tab shows all the transactions posted to the blockchain so far.

4. The tab named "contracts" will show the list of the smart contracts posted onto the blockchain.

5. The last two tabs detail any events and logs on the blockchain. Logs have details on what time the blockchain started, IP address, database paths, and so on...

Ganache can be looked upon as a GUI software that only presents a better picture of the blockchain, which is also much more readable than looking at the blockchain in a terminal window. Note that the homepage might be subject to change. Ganache all by itself cannot be used to post a transaction on the blockchain or deploy a smart contract. To do these tasks, we need to use Truffle. Both Ganache and Truffle will be in sync with each other, i.e. any transactions/smart contracts posted on Truffle will reflect on Ganache. Another benefit of using Truffle and Ganache is that we will be able to create test accounts with 100ETH in each account which will be more than enough to do any sort of testing. Note that the ETH present on the private network is not a real cryptocurrency and is only used for testing purposes. You can also create a standalone blockchain by just using Truffle.

Figure 5.1   **Screenshot of the Ganache application**

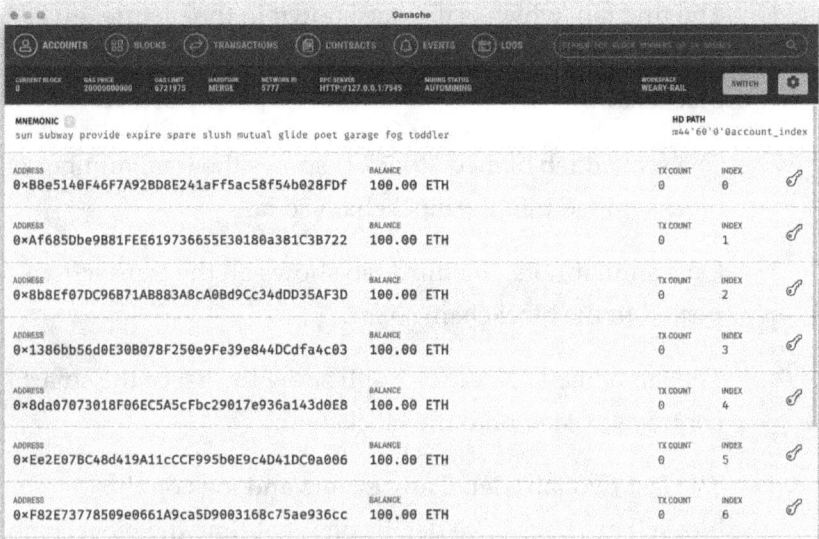

5.3 Truffle

Truffle allows us to make transactions on the blockchain. Truffle is a world-class development environment, testing framework, and asset pipeline for blockchains using the Ethereum Virtual Machine (EVM), aiming to make life as a blockchain developer easier by creating private blockchains on one's machine. With the help of a private blockchain, we can test for all the possibilities and vulnerabilities of a smart contract. On top of that, Truffle and Ganache together serve as a great learning platform for beginners in blockchain. With Truffle, you get:

Easy smart contract management: Truffle helps you write, test, and manage smart contracts (programs that run on a blockchain) all in one place.

Advanced debugging: It allows you to find and fix issues in your code by letting you pause and check the state of your program, see what variables are doing, and step through your code one line at a time.

Safe transactions with MetaMask: You can use Truffle to deploy your contracts and perform transactions safely through MetaMask (third-party Chrome browser extension), which helps protect your digital wallet information.

Run external scripts: You can use Truffle to run scripts (programs) that interact with your blockchain projects.

Interactive console: Truffle provides a command line interface where you can interact directly with your smart contracts.

Automated testing: It can automatically test your contracts to ensure they work correctly, speeding up development.

Flexible deployment: Truffle makes it easy to deploy your contracts and manage their updates across different blockchain networks.

Manage networks: It helps you deploy your contracts to various public and private blockchain networks.

Package management: Truffle integrates with NPM (a tool for managing code packages) and supports standards like ERC190 for organizing and using code.

Customizable build process: You can configure how your contracts are built and integrated into your project, making it easier to fit your specific needs.

To use Truffle, one must install Truffle onto their machine. The Truffle website offers the entire QuickStart tutorial on how to install Truffle which can be found here - https://trufflesuite.com/docs/truffle/quickstart/. Truffle has a few sample projects that come in handy for understanding the usage of the software. Using Truffle, a transaction or a smart contract can be made onto the blockchain. Once a transaction is made onto the blockchain, Ganache automatically updates the transaction on the front end. The transaction made can be viewed on both Truffle and Ganache. Unlike Ganache, which has a frontend GUI application, Truffle is run and viewed entirely on the command line. All the commands in Truffle will have to run on the command line.

A sample screenshot of Truffle which shows the same account numbers in both Ganache and Truffle is shown in Figure 5.2 and Figure 5.3.

Figure 5.2 | **Opening a truffle console from the terminal window**

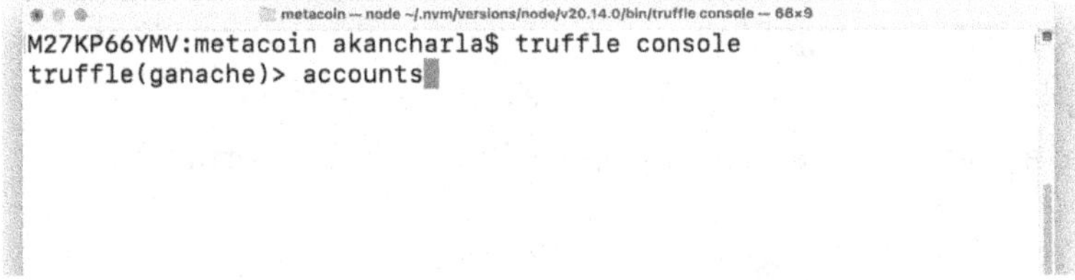

```
● ● ●          metacoin — node ~/.nvm/versions/node/v20.14.0/bin/truffle console — 68×9
M27KP66YMV:metacoin akancharla$ truffle console
truffle(ganache)> accounts
```

Figure 5.3 | **Screenshot of the Truffle console with the command "accounts" typed in**

```
● ● ●          metacoin — node ~/.nvm/versions/node/v20.14.0/bin/truffle console — 66×15
M27KP66YMV:metacoin akancharla$ truffle console
truffle(ganache)> accounts
[
  '0xB8e6140F46F7A92BD8E241aFf5ac58f54b028FDf',
  '0xAf685Dbe9B81FEE619736655E30180a381C38722',
  '0x8b8Ef07DC96B71AB883A8cA0Bd9Cc34dDD35AF3D',
  '0x1386bb56d0E30B078F250e9Fe39e844DCdfa4c03',
  '0x8da07073018F06EC5A5cFbc29017e936a143d0E8',
  '0xEe2E07BC48d419A11cCCF995b0E9c4D41DC0a006',
  '0xF82E73778509e0661A9ca5D9003168c75ae936cc',
  '0xd5E13324a1149372042C4E851e4E287e617f824C',
  '0xd5Dc8853973161C579f67Fc61092770f12eFD41F',
  '0x892b20a44390d276F7AE7F842836a087e21E7A89'
]
truffle(ganache)>
```

A Truffle console can be started in your terminal by typing in the command - "truffle console". Do not type the inverted commas though. Once the Truffle console is open, we can interact with the blockchain by various predefined commands. Notice the black colored font and the ">" symbol in the above picture. The arrow-looking symbol - ">" is where various blockchain-related commands can be typed in and processed. Multiple commands can be typed in at that particular spot on the terminal window. Depending on the command, appropriate outputs are shown. Using Web3 commands on Truffle and Ganache will allow us to send Ethereum over the network to another public address, post a smart contract onto the Ethereum network, view all the accounts in the blockchain, view the number of cryptocurrencies each account has, and much more. In the above figure, the command "accounts" was typed in and the resulting output was the displaying of all the accounts. The addresses of the account shown here are the same as the addresses in the Truffle terminal window.

You can come out of the Truffle console by pressing Ctrl + C anytime on your keyboard, which takes you outside the Truffle window and back into the terminal. You can create a bare project without smart contracts using **truffle init**, but for those that are just getting started with blockchain, you can use Truffle Boxes, which are example applications and project templates. One of the commonly used Truffle boxes is the MetaCoin project which has a basic functionality of creating a token that can be transferred between accounts. A token is discussed in detail in the upcoming sections. Steps to create a Truffle-based project are given below:

1. Before we download the MetaCoin project template, we need to create a folder/directory, otherwise, all the files will be downloaded to your home directory and will be all over the place. To create a new directory through the terminal, type in **mkdir metacoin**

Figure 5.4 | **Creating a new folder from the terminal window**

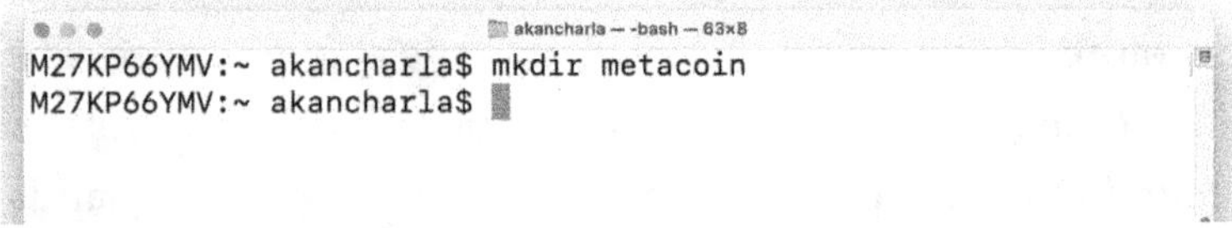

```
●  ●  ●                    akancharla — -bash — 63x8
M27KP66YMV:~ akancharla$ mkdir metacoin
M27KP66YMV:~ akancharla$
```

2. This will create a folder named metacoin. We will download the project template into that folder. Although there will be no response from the command line after the mkdir command, the folder itself has been created as long as there is no error.

3. Once the folder is created, we will have to navigate into that folder. This can be done by using one of the basic commands of the terminal – cd. Type in **"cd metacoin"** in the terminal and press <ENTER>. This cd command, short for change directory, will have the terminal point to the new folder that you have just downloaded.

Navigating into the new folder that was created

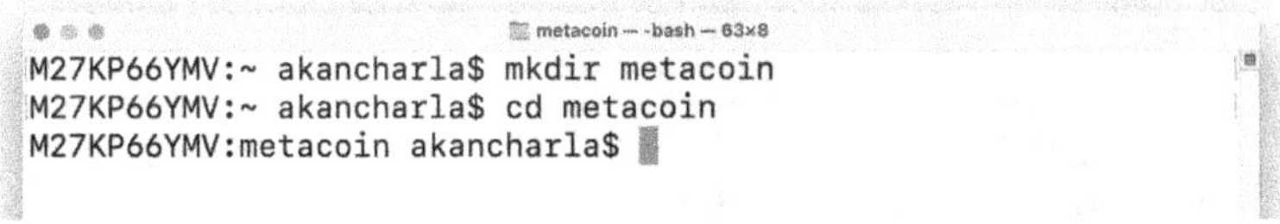

```
●  ●  ●                    metacoin — -bash — 63×8
M27KP66YMV:~ akancharla$ mkdir metacoin
M27KP66YMV:~ akancharla$ cd metacoin
M27KP66YMV:metacoin akancharla$
```

Notice that the terminal now says metacoin before the username, which implies that we are inside the metacoin directory.

4. After we have created a directory to store all the project-related files, we should be able to download the MetaCoin project template. To download the project folder, open the terminal window on your machine. Once opened, type in – `truffle unbox metacoin [PATH/TO/DIRECTORY]`.

Figure 5.6 **Navigating into the new folder**

```
●  ●  ●                    metacoin — -bash — 59×12
M27KP66YMV:~ akancharla$ cd metacoin
M27KP66YMV:metacoin akancharla$ truffle unbox metacoin
```

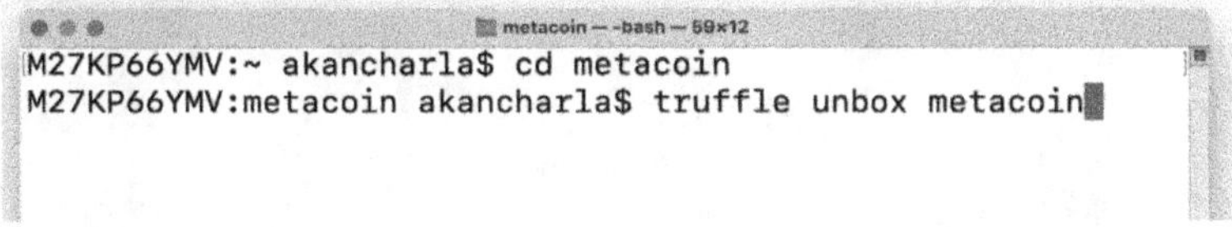

5. If the PATH/TO/DIRECTORY is ignored, the Metacoin project will be downloaded in the same directory that the terminal is pointing to right now, as shown above.

Figure 5.7   **Unboxing a sample Truffle project**

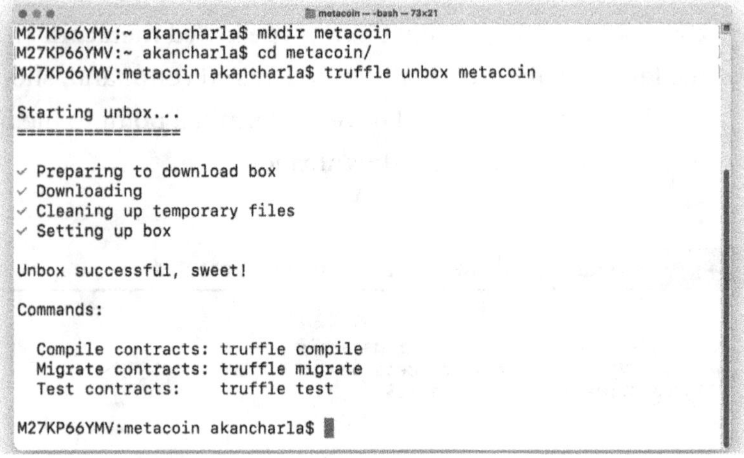

```
●  ●  ●                    metacoin — -bash — 73×21
M27KP66YMV:~ akancharla$ mkdir metacoin
M27KP66YMV:~ akancharla$ cd metacoin/
M27KP66YMV:metacoin akancharla$ truffle unbox metacoin

Starting unbox...
=================

✓ Preparing to download box
✓ Downloading
✓ Cleaning up temporary files
✓ Setting up box

Unbox successful, sweet!

Commands:

  Compile contracts: truffle compile
  Migrate contracts: truffle migrate
  Test contracts:    truffle test

M27KP66YMV:metacoin akancharla$ ▊
```

6. The unbox command will download the appropriate
    resources to run the MetaCoin project on your machine. If
    the unbox command is successful, there will be a directory
    named – metacoin, with the files necessary for creating and
    deploying a smart contract.

Figure 5.8   **Project in the Explorer/Finder window**

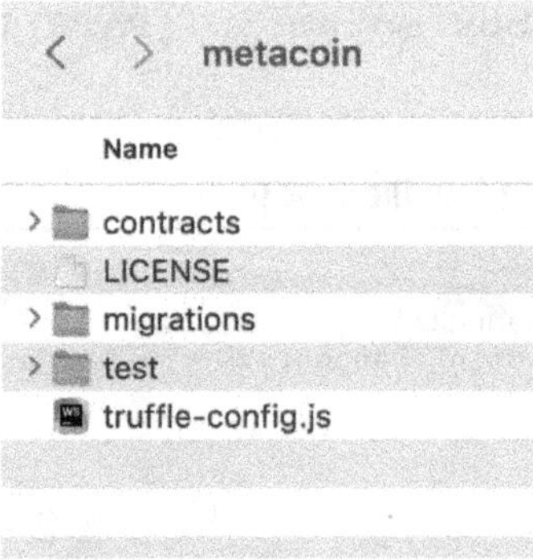

```
      ❮   ❯      metacoin

      Name

   ❯  📁 contracts
      📄 LICENSE
   ❯  📁 migrations
   ❯  📁 test
      🔲 truffle-config.js
```

7. Once the necessary files are downloaded with the unbox
    command, the folder should look more or less like the one
    shown in the above picture.

| Figure 5.9 | Checking the contents of the folder from a terminal |

```
● ● ●                          metacoin — -bash — 75×12
M27KP66YMV:metacoin akancharla$ ls
LICENSE                 migrations              truffle-config.js
contracts               test
M27KP66YMV:metacoin akancharla$ truffle migrate
```

8. "ls" is a basic Linux-based command that will show the contents of the folder as seen in the above picture.

New terms so far

- **Corda:** Corda is an open-source distributed ledger platform for businesses, developed by R3, a software company with a focus on distributed ledger technology (DLT). Corda has been designed to serve the needs of enterprise applications, including but not limited to financial services, supply chain management, healthcare, and so forth.

- **remix.ethereum.org:** Remix Online IDE (integrated development environment) is a powerful toolset for developing, deploying, debugging, and testing Ethereum and EVM-compatible smart contracts. You will have the choice of using either Remix or any simple text editor to develop a smart contract in the chapter.

- **Statically-typed:** Statically typed is a programming language characteristic in which variable types are explicitly declared and thus are determined at compile time. Notice in the example shown in the figure that the "number" variable is declared as unit256. This lets the compiler decide whether a given variable can perform the actions requested from it or not.

- **GUI:** Short form for Graphical User Interface, it is a design system that allows people to interact with electronic devices such as computers, smartphones, tablets, and other digital systems through graphical elements like windows, icons, buttons, and menus, rather than text-based interfaces such as CLI.

- **Mainnet:** The term "mainnet" is used to refer to the primary or main blockchain of any cryptocurrency, the live network that handles real trades and transfers. When you send cryptocurrency tokens to someone on the internet, you're using the main network (as opposed to its testnet or other networks for development). It is important to note here that transactions in the mainnet are final; they are "set in stone". Whenever you send a valid transaction, you are sending real money or assets to someone in the network, making it non-reversible. This addition of a new transaction to the blockchain, which is the primary use-case for the blockchain, cannot be reversed.

- **Testnet:** On the other hand is the testnet, which is a copy of the mainnet run for experimentation purposes. It's very much parallel with the real mainnet network on which the token has actual value but typically uses some "test" or fake token units that cannot be used for any real-world transactions. Testnets are used for trying out new features such as smart contracts, for testing software upgrades and other services or features like builders and developers of blockchain projects (dApps or movements such as Web3), and users and testers

> trying out new software on the blockchain without
> clogging up the actual mainnet network and most
> importantly, without wasting real funds. Anyone
> can obtain the test tokens for free through faucets or
> developer tools.

So far, we have downloaded a project template from the Truffle website using the terminals via some basic commands. The next steps describe how to start Truffle and how Ganache and Truffle can work together in sync.

1. Once in the directory of metacoin, inside the terminal, type in "truffle test" which will test for successful connection with the Solidity compiler and a couple of other tests.

2. Once tested, type in "truffle compile", which will compile all the smart contracts present in the metacoin folder and are tested for any errors in the smart contracts.

3. The in-built smart contracts that were downloaded directly from the project template will not have any errors, and this part should usually be error-free.

4. Once compiled, we can upload the smart contracts to the blockchain. The creation of a smart contract and uploading of the same can be done using the command "truffle migrate". This will compile the pre-written smart contracts in the metacoin project template directory and deploy the smart contracts onto the blockchain created by Ganache. Make sure that Ganache is also up and running. The following two screenshots show the output for the migrate command.

Figure 5.10 Migrating the contracts from the Truffle window

```
metacoin — -bash — 76x26
M27KP66YMV:metacoin akancharla$ truffle migrate

Compiling your contracts...
===========================
> Compiling ./contracts/ConvertLib.sol
> Compiling ./contracts/MetaCoin.sol
> Artifacts written to /Users/akancharla/metacoin/build/contracts
> Compiled successfully using:
   - solc: 0.8.13+commit.abaa5c0e.Emscripten.clang


Starting migrations...
======================
> Network name:    'ganache'
> Network id:      5777
> Block gas limit: 6721975 (0x6691b7)


1_deploy_contracts.js
=====================

   Deploying 'ConvertLib'
   ----------------------
   > transaction hash:    0x80a9869a9080f6221986d2a706e1c6a85b2670e97cccb54b
8e02a00a60ecd37c
   > Blocks: 0            Seconds: 0
```

Figure 5.11 Migrating the contracts from the Truffle window

```
metacoin — -bash — 81x30
   --------
   * Contract: MetaCoin <--> Library: ConvertLib (at address: 0x5790adBdaa993C999
d9834c06820ab4d20bac7e5)

   Deploying 'MetaCoin'
   --------------------
   > transaction hash:    0x758bf694ba5b86b65af022dc968b6d0d49632d807af32e8af43b6
025b7e46568
   > Blocks: 0            Seconds: 0
   > contract address:    0x2dA8B3Bc12069e56546eAD1C36d202cC6cEDD8be
   > block number:        2
   > block timestamp:     1730527713
   > account:             0xB8e5140F46F7A92BD8E241aFf5ac58f54b028FDf
   > balance:             99.998105632065943366
   > gas used:            416594 (0x65b52)
   > gas price:           3.270752661 gwei
   > value sent:          0 ETH
   > total cost:          0.001362575934056634 ETH

   > Saving artifacts
   -------------------------------------
   > Total cost:     0.001894367934056634 ETH

Summary
=======
> Total deployments:   2
> Final cost:          0.001894367934056634 ETH


M27KP66YMV:metacoin akancharla$ █
```

5. Switch to the Ganache application and you can see the same two contract transactions being present on Ganache.

Figure 5.12.1 Checking the status in Ganache application

Figure 5.12.2 Checking the status in Ganache application

6. By typing the Truffle console command, we can access the Truffle console in which the blockchain commands can be processed.

Figure 5.13 Accessing the Ganache console

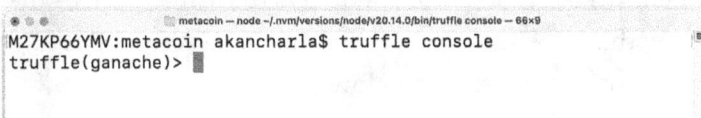

```
metacoin — node ~/.nvm/versions/node/v20.14.0/bin/truffle console — 66×9
M27KP66YMV:metacoin akancharla$ truffle console
truffle(ganache)>
```

7. Inside the console, various Web3-based commands can be typed in and the results are obtained on the same screen after preceding the <Enter> key. For example, go ahead and type in Web3 in the console, and you should see an output similar to the one shown in the figure below. The output given by the "web3" command is too big, hence only a part of the output is shown in the figure.

Figure 5.14   **Typing in 'web3' command in Ganache console**

```
●  ●  ●              metacoin — node ~/.nvm/versions/node/v20.14.0/bin/truffle console — 09×24
M27KP66YMV:metacoin akancharla$ truffle console
truffle(ganache)> web3
Web3Shim {
  currentProvider: [Getter/Setter],
  _requestManager: RequestManager {
    provider: HttpProvider {
      withCredentials: undefined,
      timeout: 0,
      headers: undefined,
      agent: undefined,
      connected: false,
      host: 'http://127.0.0.1:7545',
      httpAgent: [Agent],
      send: [Function (anonymous)],
      request: [Function: bound modifiedRequest] AsyncFunction,
      _alreadyWrapped: true
    },
    providers: {
      WebsocketProvider: [Function: WebsocketProvider],
      HttpProvider: [Function: HttpProvider],
      IpcProvider: [Function: IpcProvider]
    },
    subscriptions: Map(0) {}
  },
```

8. If we look back into the Ganache application, the Blocks tab should show all the respective blocks that have been added to the blockchain so far. The same blocks are present in the Truffle console as well. Truffle and Ganache are both pointing to the same blockchain. Switch back to the Truffle console and type in "web3.eth.getBlock "web3.eth. getBlock(4)", the output shown is the same block as the one that is being shown in the Ganache screen. Both the screenshots are shown below:

| Figure 5.15 | Ganache application screenshot of block 4. |

| Figure 5.16 | Truffle application screenshot of block 4. |

Since we are using a private blockchain, we don't need to worry about the amount of currency we have on Ganache as everything is for testing purposes. The status of transactions on the blockchain can be seen in the above figure, indicating the transactions made by Truffle. Note how the transactions clearly indicate that they are for contract creation. Likewise, if currency is to be transferred from one account to another, it can be done via Truffle as well.

5.4 How to Write Your Own Smart Contract

To begin with, you can use the Metacoin example and start making changes to the smart contract to make it your own. In the folder of Metacoin, there should be a sub-folder named contracts. Under the contract folder, open the file named Metacoin.sol which is the smart contract. The .sol extension for a file implies that the file contains a program that can be read and executed by a solidity compiler. As writing a new smart contract from scratch requires programming knowledge and is out of the scope of this book, the following website contains an in-depth view of smart contracts and all related programming constructs - https://docs.soliditylang. org/. Some sample smart contracts (the files have an extension of .sol and can be opened with any text editors like Notepad) are included in the supplementary materials for this book -

- IdentityVerification.sol - Smart contract that can be used to verify identification

- RealEstate.sol - A smart contract that keeps track of the ownership in real estate

- Voting.sol - A smart contract that can be used for voting purposes

- ShipmentTracking.sol - Contract to track the shipment from the owner to the current location

- SimpleToken.sol - A smart contract that represents a basic token on the Ethereum blockchain

- Simple.sol - A basic smart contract that stores a message onto a blockchain and also has functions to retrieve the same message.

5.5 ICO, ITO, and Crowd sale

5.5.1 ICO

ICO, also short for Initial Coin Offerings, refers to raising funds for a new cryptocurrency or any other blockchain-related project. It's similar to an IPO in which funds are received when a new company ventures into the stock market. The parties giving the funds in an IPO are usually given a stake in the stock market. Likewise, in ICO, the parties giving funds to raise a new cryptocurrency are given a stake in the project. ICO is an unregulated means of raising funds. Indeed, ICOs are so unregulated that anyone can run an ICO.

Several ICOs have resulted in a good return to their investors, but the vast majority of ICOs ended up performing poorly, or in some cases, fraudulently. ICOs mostly rely on white papers generated by the project creators that are made available to the investors. As the entire process of ICO is unregulated and dependent on a completely new project, a high degree of caution is advised for investors. It's the job of the investors to investigate the project and determine the worth of investing in an ICO.

If the money raised by the investors in ICO is not sufficient enough to continue the project, usually the money is returned to the investors. On the other hand, if the money requirements are met, the money would then be used to start the project.

5.5.2 ITO

Initial Token Offerings (ITOs) are the same as ICOs (Initial Coin Offerings), the main difference being that ICOs are done to enable buying a new cryptocurrency through a tech document on the so-called white paper, whereas ITOs are done for projects that are useful as proven and work for it. It is mostly done to raise awareness about the project among the users on the blockchain.

5.5.3 Crowdsales

The cryptocurrency ICO, or crowd sale, is a public offering for funding a new cryptocurrency, or pretty much any digital asset you can think of including NFTs. Crowd sales attract large amounts of crowds just because they can buy the new coin at a very low cost.

5.6 Solidity

Solidity is a curly-braces programming language, statically-typed, designed for writing smart contracts for Ethereum. A programming language is a lexicon and syntax for telling a computer – potentially a distributed one on a network of computers – to do things, and Solidity is a programming language. The below figure shows a simple smart contract displaying the use of curly braces as a means of creating a block.

Figure 5.17   A very simple smart contract written in Solidity

```
1    // SPDX-License-Identifier: GPL-3.0
2
3    pragma solidity >=0.8.2 <0.9.0;
4
5  ⌄ /**
6    * @title Storage
7    * @dev Store & retrieve value in a variable
8    * @custom:dev-run-script ./scripts/deploy_with_ethers.ts
9    */
10 ⌄ contract Storage {
11
12       uint256 number;
13
14 ⌄    /**
15       * @dev Store value in variable
16       * @param num value to store
17       */
18 ⌄    function store(uint256 num) public {      🔋 22514 gas
19           number = num;
20       }
21
22 ⌄    /**
23       * @dev Return value
24       * @return value of 'number'
25       */
26 ⌄    function retrieve() public view returns (uint256){   🔋 2410 gas
27           return number;
28       }
```

We will get into line-by-line details of the above program:

- Line 3 - This is where we can provide which version of Solidity to be used to compile our program. Due to the fast pace of changes that are happening to blockchain, there will be significant changes in the versions of Solidity.

- Line 10 - Name of smart contract to be declared

- Line 12 - Declaring a variable named number, which will allow us to store values in that shoebox.

- Line 18:20 - A function defined as store will assign a value in "num" to "number".

- Line 26:28 - A function defined as retrieve will return the value present in the number.

- Line 29 - A closing parentheses matching the opening parenthesis in Line 10

5.7 Smart Contracts – The Way it Should Be

Now consider the case of a smart contract – which is in essence a self-executing contract in which the terms and agreements between the buyer and the seller are written verbatim into lines of code. That code and the terms of the contract are stored and replicated onto a blockchain network. Smart contracts are a collection of rules that the code follows when a user makes a function call within the smart contract. It can also be thought of as a self-executing tap of code that will automatically execute when conditions are met, with those conditions/agreements/rules being established while code is constructed. An easy way to write/deploy a smart contract onto a private blockchain is to simply use remix.ethereum.org which allows you to deploy a smart contract on the private blockchain and also debug a smart contract.

Smart contracts, which allow a block to contain computer code, have brought blockchain far beyond cryptocurrency investment, adding an entire world of real-time applications to blockchain architecture.

To be usable, smart contracts must first be deployed over the blockchain. Not all blockchains support smart contracts, but almost certainly many of the blockchains that have come to market in the past year or so support smart contracts. Some of the more popular smart contract-supporting blockchains are, in alphabetical order: – Ethereum – Hyperledger Fabric – Corda – Stellar – RootStock. Smart contracts have the potential to revolutionize many different domains as they can be used to simplify or automate processes and reduce intermediaries. For example, smart contracts have already been deployed in diverse use cases including supply chain management, real estate, and financial services.

5.8 Account types

In Ethereum, there are two types of accounts:

1. **EOA (Externally Owned Accounts):** An EOA is an account created on the blockchain and has no associated code alongside it. EOA is controlled using private keys and can send and receive transactions. To send money from EOA, a private key is needed. On the other hand, a public address is enough for receiving money from an EOA

2. **Contract Accounts:** Contract accounts are created when a smart contract is deployed onto the Blockchain. Contract accounts have an associated code and execute any transaction received from EOA. Rules can be written in the smart contract that will allow the transfer of funds to an EOA.

5.9 Digital Assets

Before blockchain, digital assets have always been referred to as items like data, images, video, and audio that can be stored on a computer. After blockchain, the meaning of digital assets has obtained a much broader definition. A digital asset includes entities that can be created/stored primarily using blockchain technology. Also note that the digital assets are not stored on the blockchain, but rather blocked as a means to secure the transaction related to digital assets. Usually, the digital asset itself is stored in a distributed network called Interplanetary File System often referred to as IPFS. The most common of the digital assets is photos. There can be many digital assets stored with the blockchain such as pictures, videos, documents, audio, email, animations, metadata, etc. These digital assets have become desirable in recent times due to their various characteristics like transparency, security, and immutability. They have job applications in areas like financial transactions, supply chain management, and the representation of physical assets.

Key-Terms

Crowd-sale	Digital Assets	Ganache	ICO
ITO	Metacoin	Smart-contract	Solidity
Truffle			

Quiz

1. **What are the different types of accounts in the Ethereum blockchain? Select all that apply.**

   a. Token accounts

   b. Externally Owned Accounts

   c. Contract Accounts

   d. All of the above

2. **The following are used to create rules and automatically execute the said rules when the conditions are met:**

   a. Addresses

   b. Smart contracts

   c. Blockchain

   d. Currency

3. **A picture when stored as a digital asset is placed on the blockchain.**

   a. True

   b. False

4. **Where are the digital assets usually stored?**

   a. Blockchain

   b. Block

   c. IPFS

   d. Smart contract

5. **What is the full form of ITO?**

   a. Initial Technology Offering

   b. Initial Token Offering

   c. Initial Token Organization

   d. Initial Technology Organization

6. **What is the purpose of using Truffle in conjunction with Ganache?**

   a. To create a public blockchain

   b. To develop decentralized applications

   c. To facilitate digital currency transactions

   d. To deploy smart contracts

7. **Ganache and Truffle can be used to create a private blockchain.**

   a. True

   b. False

8. Which of the following can be stored as a digital asset on a blockchain?

a. Pictures

b. Videos

c. Metadata

d. Audio

e. All of the above

9. ERC-721 is a type of protocol used primarily for creating:

a. Smart contracts

b. NFT

c. Blockchain account

d. Blockchain

10. Which of the following is not mentioned as a use case for digital tokens in the text?

a. Real estate investments

b. Trading digital assets

c. Transferring data files

d. Collectibles

Answers	1 – b, c	2 – b	3 – b	4 – c	5 – b
	6 – d	7 – a	8 –e	9 – b	10 – c

Chapter Summary

◆ Ganache and Truffle are third-party software that helps us test our smart contracts on blockchain before deploying a smart contract on the Ethereum blockchain.

◆ Ganache and Truffle are based on the Ethereum blockchain.

◆ Smart contracts help create the value of digital tokens.

◆ The programming language used to write smart contracts on the Ethereum blockchain is Solidity.

◆ Initial Coin Offerings (ICO) are another way to crowdfund a new cryptocurrency or a blockchain-related project.

◆ Ethereum has two types of accounts: Externally Owned Accounts (EOA) and Contract Accounts.

Chapter 6

Implementing Blockchain Projects

Designing or planning to incorporate a blockchain into your project is not all about knowing the technical paradigms. We have a rough draft of the technical aspects of blockchain from Chapter 5; in this chapter, we will dive deeper into criteria that are to be taken into consideration to implement a blockchain project or to incorporate a blockchain into a legacy system. We will also look at various case studies and then study them to grasp knowledge from these different real-life blockchain projects. Finally, we will conclude this chapter by introducing some of the well-known Hyperledger projects.

After studying this chapter, you will be able to:

- Create a roadmap that will help you launch your blockchain initiative

- Understand the key considerations for selecting a blockchain platform

- Discover the different types of testing that is to be performed on a blockchain project

- Understand the various projects and the scope of these projects in the Hyperledger foundation

- Learn about the security considerations that need to be taken in a blockchain

6.1 Project Planning and Feasibility

Planning and feasibility consideration are critical elements for a successful and sustainable blockchain project. With this in mind, the introduction of blockchain within organizations and public bodies likely starts with some clear objectives and an understanding of potential use cases – which is the focus of this section. How do you establish clear objectives and use cases? How can you run a feasibility study to confirm the validity of the project? What are the core steps to follow to run an accurate feasibility study? How can you assess the technical feasibility, the economic feasibility, and the operational feasibility – while carefully considering stakeholders' requirements and the related risks? This section takes a structured approach to feasibility assessment by providing a checklist for evaluating the various dimensions of feasibility. It then carefully walks through the key considerations of each aspect and tries to answer the questions that arise about feasibility type. All these considerations need to be fully detailed and mapped out to help organizations create a roadmap that is very likely to succeed with clear objectives and use cases that are economically feasible and operationally valid. Blockchain is not a solution for every problem out there; there are a lot of cases where introducing blockchain into the mix would not pay off in the long run. As much as blockchain has garnered so much attention over the past decade, there are scenarios where it will be a good fit and scenarios where it won't. That being said, project planning should be the first thing to consider and some key points that need to be addressed are highlighted in the next few subsections.

6.1.1.Defining the project scope

Clear objectives: What problem is the blockchain-based project aiming to address? For example, consider a supply chain industry that is trying to address the problem of transparency and reduce fraud in the system by adding the traceability feature. This is a valid and clear objective for which blockchain is most likely the correct choice. Consider the same supply chain industry where the problem they are trying to address is an issue of high-volume and high-frequency transactions. In this case, blockchain will not be the correct fit as blockchain systems typically have slower transaction speeds.

Use case identification: Identify and describe the specific use case(s) for blockchain applications.

6.1.2 Feasibility study

Feasibility: Determine if something can be done through practical judgment.

Technical Feasibility: Assess whether the requisite technology and resources are available and evaluate how well they would support the project.

Economic feasibility: Look for expected costs and potential economic benefits. This might be shown through cost-benefit or ROI estimates.

Operational feasibility: Consider if the organization can operate the blockchain project.

6.1.3 Stakeholder analysis

Identify stakeholders: Draw up a list of all those who will be affected by or are interested in the project, from developers (the program creators) to users, regulators, and investors. Creating a rough draft of stakeholders will give you an estimate as to how much budget you can roughly expect to get funded for this blockchain project.

Stakeholder requirements: Gather and document the requirements and expectations of each stakeholder group.

6.1.4 Risk assessment

Risk Identification: Identify potential risks, including technical, financial, regulatory, and operational risks.

Risk mitigation strategies: Lessons identified by participants must be translated into strategies that would help workers avoid, eliminate, or mitigate risks. Identified risks should be mitigated through appropriate strategies like contingency plans, backup systems, and other measures.

6.1.5 Project Timeline and Milestones

Timeline development: Create a detailed project timeline, outlining key phases and milestones.

Milestone definitions: Define what constitutes a milestone and the criteria for successful completion.

6.1.6 Resource planning

Human resources: Identify skills for the project when considering employees and freelancers who could contribute to the project. We need a blockchain developer, project manager, and legal advisor for this project.

Available financial resources: This is an estimate of how much money is available for the project in terms of development costs, operational expenses, and contingency funds.

Technical resources: List the technical resources needed, such as hardware, software, and development tools.

6.1.7 Regulatory and legal considerations

Compliance requirements: Identify relevant regulations and compliance requirements that the project must adhere to.

Legal aspects: Assess the legal issues that arise due to the project (user privacy, intellectual property, contract enforcement, etc).

6.1.8 Success criteria

Specify success parameters: Clearly define the metrics of success that will be measured, such as speed of transactions, number of users adopting the project, and costs saved.

Performance benchmarks: Set performance benchmarks to measure progress and keep the project on track.

6.1.9 Decision-making framework

Go/No-Go decision script: Write a go/no-go decision script that can be modified based on the results of the feasibility study.

Continuous evaluation: Implement a process for continuous evaluation and reassessment throughout the project lifecycle.

6.2 Choosing the Right Blockchain Platform

Choosing the right blockchain platform for your blockchain project is critically important, but which one should you choose? And why is it important to do this part of the process well? Blockchain platforms are available, with very diverse features, capabilities, and constraints. At this point, you already have some idea about what your blockchain project will need, so there is a whole set of questions that we can ask about any given blockchain platform. In this section, we summarise what a blockchain platform is, summarise the most promising solutions on the market, and look at the key criteria that you want to factor in when choosing the right blockchain for your project. This will lay the groundwork for your decision. Some key points to note before you decide which is the potential blockchain platform that can be worth looking into your project are highlighted in the following subsections.

6.2.1 Understanding different blockchain platforms

Distinguishing between public and private blockchains and being able to provide a comparison between public vs. private blockchains such as Bitcoin, Ethereum, Hyperledger Fabric, R3 Corda, etc. should be at the top of the list. Trying to differentiate between public vs. private blockchains is one of the most important and challenging questions in the blockchain ecosystem. Describe the differences and similarities in detail, comparing the strengths and weaknesses of each type. Explain the relevant use cases for each type, while also discussing their main limitations. Also, consider adding consortium to the mix as well, given that consortium acts as a middle ground between public and private blockchains where a ranging number of organizations are in charge of a blockchain network.

6.2.2 Consensus and scalability

To understand if a given blockchain platform could cater to your application, read and analyze the consensus mechanisms such as PoW for the high-security and decentralized network but high-energy consumption, PoS for a more energy-efficient and scalable solution, and PBFT for high-throughput and low-latency for permissioned network. Some noteworthy points to be taken into consideration in to decide whether the consensus algorithm selected is the correct one or not are:

1. Check the network's scalability to see if it can handle the growth

2. Security features such as encryption and consensus

3. Performance indicators like speed and latency of the transactions

4. Need to interoperate with existing systems and with other blockchain networks

5. Smart contract support and relevant programming languages such as Solidity for Ethereum and Chaincode for Hyperledger Fabric (we will dive deeper into Chaincode in the later sections of this chapter).

6.2.3 Evaluating popular blockchain platforms

Most of the popular blockchains have already made a name out there and have their respective areas in which they demonstrated their usefulness. Some of them are listed below along with the strengths and the use cases they are commonly known for:

Hyperledger Fabric

Strengths: Permissioned network, modular architecture, high customizability, strong privacy, and confidentiality features

Use cases: Supply chain, finance, healthcare

Ethereum

Strengths: Decentralized, strong developer community, support for complex smart contracts

Use cases: Decentralized finance (DeFi), tokenization, decentralized applications (DApps)

R3 Corda

Strengths: Designed for financial services, strong focus on privacy, interoperability with existing financial systems

Use cases: Banking, insurance, trade finance

Quorum

Strengths: Enterprise-focused version of Ethereum, permissioned network, privacy enhancements Use cases: Enterprise solutions, financial services

Polkadot

Strengths: Interoperability between blockchains, scalability, shared security

Use cases: Multi-chain networks, cross-chain applications

6.2.4 Cost Considerations

Set-up costs: What are the set-up costs for this network blockchain– hardware, software, and development?

Maintenance and operational costs: Calculate how much it would cost to run the network on an ongoing basis, including costs for running nodes, updating and maintaining them, and how much technical support is required.

Transaction fees: Are there transaction fees and, if yes, how will they be built into the project budget?

6.2.5 Legal and regulatory compliance

Data privacy regulations: Make sure the platform is GDPR*, CCPA*, or other applicable privacy laws compliant.

Sector-specific regulations: Get compliant with rules or regulations that apply only to your industry, such as financial services or health care.

6.2.6 Platform Ecosystem and Community Support

Developer community: Measure the active user base and participation level in the developer community. That can be a good indication of the longevity and support of the platform.

Third-party integrations: Look for third-party tools and integrations that enhance the functionality of the platform. For example, MetaMask (wallet integration), Chainlink* (oracle services), IBM Blockchain (enterprise integration), ERC-20 (token standard), and so on.

Documentation: Check that the platform has plenty of documentation and guides to access and learn about. The documentation on Solidity is very detailed and is always up-to-date with the most recent developments.

6.2.7 Making the final decision

Pilot testing: Shortlisted platforms need to be tested to measure how they perform, their scalability, and ease of integration.

Stakeholder input: Obtain feedback from key stakeholders regarding what would be useful to them, and whether the choice would be appropriate by meeting their requirements and expectations.

New terms so far

- **GDPR:** The GDPR is a regulation by which the European Union (EU) protects the personal data and privacy of EU citizens within the EU. It applies to all companies processing the data of subjects residing in the EU, regardless of the company's location.

- **CCPA:** The CCPA is a statute of the state of California, US, that expands privacy rights and protections for consumers, or more specifically, the consumers of the state. It covers businesses that process residents' personal information that exceeds certain thresholds.

- **Chainlink:** Chainlink is an Oracle network that allows smart contracts on various blockchains to securely access external data, APIs, and other off-chain resources. Oracles connect the real world to blockchains and therefore carry the real-world data that's used as inputs to activate smart contracts when certain external conditions are met.

6.3 Integrating Blockchain with Existing Systems

While it may not be news to folks who are already familiar with blockchain, it is useful to document why and how it makes sense for organizations to try to link blockchain technology to their existing, old-economy enterprise systems. The benefits of integrating blockchain are many, but they boil down to a few key factors and address several critical problems confronting any modern enterprise.

6.3.1 Significance of integration

Greater transparency and immutability: One of blockchain's strengths is its distributed ledger technology that generates an open, immutable, and permanent record for any transaction. When blockchain is combined with other technological solutions, the resulting increased transparency can be used to benefit an organization's supply chains and financial flows, as well as its internal operations. This would greatly reduce disagreements between businesses and their suppliers, simplify audits, and increase trust among consumers and stakeholders.

Increased security: The security of blockchain comes from its cryptographic techniques and its decentralized architecture. The risks of data breaches, fraud, and unauthorized access come down by integrating blockchain into the legacy systems which more often are centralized. It makes information security-oriented and allows the data to be stored and transmitted securely. Blockchain maintains data in a state that is untampered and auditable.

Efficiency gains: When blockchain is integrated, trust is automated and intermediaries aren't needed In particular, smart contracts enable conditions to be baked into transactions, which are then automatically executed (e.g., a smart refrigerator ordering an online grocery delivery as soon as your cheese supply runs out), thereby speeding up transaction processing and reducing administrative overheads. Financial services, supply chain management, and healthcare will be just a few areas that'll see big improvements by bringing in blockchain into their already well-established systems.

Interoperability and data integrity: Blockchain creates a single source of truth, deterring malicious interference, which is vital for data integrity. In addition, most businesses operate harmoniously with connected business networks and stakeholders, so the industry at large benefits from data being consistent and readily accessible across all connected networks, a use case that often requires or demands interoperability.

Innovation and competitive advantage: Companies that embrace blockchain will occupy a leading position in technological innovation. Companies that use blockchain's value in coming up with new businesses, services, or dApps have the potential to be industry trailblazers.

Compliance: Blockchain's transparency and audit capability also assist organizations in complying with stricter regulatory requirements. As all transactions and data exchanges are integrated into this system, transactions become actualized accordingly, reducing compliance costs and risks of regulatory penalties.

For instance, IBM's Food Trust[16] , blockchain platform can tie in with the legacy supply chain management systems used by all the firms involved in bringing food – from producer to processor to packager to shipper to grocery store to consumer – to create a more efficient and perfectly secure system. Suppliers can largely leave legacy systems as is, integrating them only with blockchains to remove inefficiencies, weed out fraud, and reassure the people along supply chains that everyone is playing on the up-and-up. Another example is Ripple, the company behind the XRP cryptocurrency which sells blockchain-based payment solutions that work alongside existing banking infrastructure to settle cross-border transactions in real-time with end-to-end visibility and lower fees than traditional cross-border payments. Banks and other financial institutions can integrate RippleNet with their legacy systems to speed up global transactions.

---

16. *IBM Food Trust, IBM,* accessed September 8, 2024, https://www.ibm.com/products/supply-chain-intelligence-suite/food-trust.

6.3.2 Integration patterns

As blockchain technology is now being applied to a growing range of research areas, usually involving independent networks, integration patterns have become particularly relevant. They allow us to apply a collection of tried and tested design patterns to the challenge of expanding the scope and efficiency of decentralized networks. Sidechains, state channels, and interoperability protocols are three typical examples.

Sidechains

Sidechains are a layering solution to help scale blockchains (that is, make them many times faster) and increase interoperability between them via the development of parallel private blockchains that run on top of another blockchain (referred to from here as the mainchain or main blockchain). Sidechains allow scalability off the main chain, thus avoiding the problems of congestion and slow performance associated with too much on-chain storage. After registering the transactions on-chain, they process the same transactions off-chain, freeing up the main blockchain and increasing total throughput while also relieving congestion in the network. Scaling solutions enable common applications like use case token transactions (gaming tokens, asset tokenization) to work at high speed and low cost without sacrificing the performance of the main blockchain.

State channels

State channels allow safe off-chain transactions by making periodic updates on the chain, while also addressing the problem of slow speeds. The main idea behind these off-chain channels of interaction is that they enable an agreed-upon amount of interaction between the participants which will be reflected (every so often) as a new state on the main (or base) chain. Unlike a traditional standalone blockchain system, where all the transactions are validated and settled on on-chain, the transactions within a blockchain-integrated system using state channels are validated off-chain, which leads to a drastic reduction in transaction costs and an increase in transaction speed. State channels still use the same consensus mechanism to settle disputes or finalize states, if a dispute emerges. State channels are proven to improve scalability by reducing the number of transactions that need to be processed on-chain, which allows for higher transaction throughput on the blockchain network. Similar to side chains, state channels can be implemented for applications requiring high-frequency interactions, including micropayments, gaming, or places where assets are exchanged in real time.

Interoperability

Finally, and also relevant to the theme of interoperability, there are interoperability protocols such as Interledger, which essentially enable the networks to talk to each other, and thus allow for the transfer of assets and data within separate ecosystems. Just like the previous two integration patterns, Interoperability mechanisms make blockchain networks scalable by letting them specialize in specific functionalities while staying interoperable with other networks. This means that blockchains that need to focus on payments can put the entire focus on payments, while blockchains that need to focus on smart contracts can put all the focus toward making better smart contract algorithms. Together, all these integration patterns point to an ongoing evolution of blockchain technology, which, despite all the hype surrounding cryptocurrency, will eventually be used for more humble applications as well, including finance, supply chain management, logistics, and intermediation.

6.4 Testing and Deployment

The successful implementation of any blockchain project relies on rigorous testing. Ensure that blockchain deployments are executed with the utmost rigor to meet the demands of an industry. As companies increasingly incorporate provably secure, distributed blockchain projects into their business workflows, the need to ensure that these blockchain projects meet specifications for performance, functionality, and security at scale grows in significance. In this section, we will define how robust and secure blockchain development can be achieved with strict and thoughtful testing strategies and strategic deployment. Testing these projects for both functional and security specifications for provable security is crucial. Doing so ensures that every block in a chain of events meets the highest criteria for authenticity, trust, and operability. Testnet blockchains like the one that we developed in Chapter 5 can be used rigorously to do the testing before the smart contracts or transactions are posted on the realnet blockchain which involves finances. The key objectives of this section are to explain how to achieve highly robust, scalable, and secure blockchain deployments while combating the inherent problems that arise in the blockchain world. As companies transition into the future with blockchain deployments, we believe it will be paramount for them to know not only the risks involved but also the best strategies for mitigating them.

6.4.1 Types of testing

Here's a comprehensive guide on the types of testing you should run on your blockchain project. The following table can be generalized for almost all software projects and not just blockchain-related projects.

Testing type	Purpose	Approach	Tools	Example
Unit testing	Validating the functionality of individual components or functions that are in isolation	Write and execute test cases for each function or method within smart contracts or other modules.	Ethereum - Truffle Hardhat. Hyperledger Fabric - Fabric SDK testing frameworks R3 Corda - JUnit	Write a simple test case to check if the transfers are executed on tokens correctly whilst updating the balances as well.
Integration testing	Ensuring that different components or services work together as intended.	Testing interactions between smart contracts, blockchain nodes, and external systems.	Ethereum - Mocha with Chai for JavaScript testing. Hyperledger Fabric - Hyperledger Composer for integration scenarios. R3 Corda - Corda Integration Test Framework	Verify that a transaction that was recorded by one node is being correctly propagated to all other nodes.
System testing	To test the end-to-end blockchain system to check for all functionality	Conduct end-to-end testing, covering the entire workflow and interactions within the network.	Custom scripts and test suites that simulate real-world scenarios	For example, in a blockchain-integrated supply-chain application, we can test an entire flow, from creating an order to receiving a confirmation of the delivered goods.

Testing type	Purpose	Approach	Tools	Example
Performance testing	To measure the throughput, latency, and scalability of the blockchain network	Simulate high transaction loads and measure the system's response.	Hyperledger Caliper: A benchmarking tool for blockchain performance testing. Ethereum TestRPC/Ganache: For local testing and performance measurement.	Measure how many transactions per second (TPS) the network can handle under different conditions.
Security testing	Identify and mitigate vulnerabilities in the blockchain application and network.	Conduct penetration testing, vulnerability assessments, and code reviews.	MythX: For Ethereum smart contract security analysis. Hyperledger Fabric Security Testing Tools: Various tools and scripts are provided by the Hyperledger community.	Test for common vulnerabilities such as reentrancy attacks, integer overflows, and unauthorized access.
UAT (User acceptance testing)	Validate that the blockchain solution meets end-user requirements and expectations	Engage real users to test the system and provide feedback on usability and functionality.	Custom user testing scripts, feedback forms, and surveys. Alpha releases will help release the project for a specified set of users and test for any defects in the system.	Have supply chain managers use the blockchain system to track shipments and provide feedback on ease of use and efficiency.

These various forms of testing will help ensure that, once developed, your blockchain-based application is robust, secure, and ready to go live. Each type of test helps address different areas, ensuring complete coverage and making it easier to resolve issues early in development.

6.5 Case Studies of Successful Blockchain Implementations

This section looks deeper into how blockchain can be deployed in the real world and talks about implementations in the finance and banking industry, supply chain management, healthcare services, property transactions, government operations, and the energy sector. We will go through these implementations, looking at a brief overview of the problem being solved, how blockchain can help, advantages captured through the project, challenges encountered, and also what can be learned for any organization looking at leveraging blockchain to solve a problem, augment an existing process, or create some value. Below are only a few of the vast number of successful case studies in blockchain.

6.5.1 Financial Services

Consensys Quorum

Originally developed by J.P.Morgan, and later acquired by Consensys, Quorum is an enterprise-variant of the Ethereum blockchain. Quorum was created by J.P.Morgan in 2016, by soft forking Ethereum blockchain. Quorum, being a private blockchain does not have any cryptocurrency associated with the blockchain itself. Quorum does contain a stablecoin (JPM) which will facilitate transfers between companies that are using Quorum. Only approved members can join the network and the blockchain ensures that sensitive financial information is only accessible to authorized parties. Unlike the public blockchains that use PoW consensus algorithms that use high energy, Quorum uses consensus mechanisms like Raft and Istanbul BFT.

Santander's One Pay FX (Ripple)

Santander launched One Pay FX, a blockchain-based international payment service using Ripple Interledger Protocol (ILP), which allows retail customers to send and receive money internationally in real-time via a mobile phone. Initially, the platform was available in four countries – Spain, the UK, Brazil, and Poland. One Pay was designed to make payments much faster, cheaper, and more transparent than the standard bank wire transfer under the guise of near-instantaneous transactions with real-time tracking and full disclosure of fees. One Pay FX also reduces the friction caused by the numerous legacy financial systems involved in international payments by aggregating the world's payment systems into one global financial network. Customers interact with Santander's app to send payments, receive money, or check their balance. The blockchain-powered service provides a secure, tamper-proof transaction experience with competitive exchange rates. Nevertheless, Santander One Pay FX, despite its originality, has generated only a modest pickup from customers today, partly due to a lack of clear incentives to adopt the blockchain payments solution, regulatory hurdles, and system integration quirks.

6.5.2. Supply Chain Management

Walmart and IBM's Food Trust

Walmart partnered with IBM to enhance food traceability using blockchain technology from the Hyperledger Fabric platform. To test out whether the traceability system works as planned, Walmart and its technology partner IBM ran two proof of concept projects. One project revolved around mangoes that Walmart sells in the US and the other project around tracking pork that Walmart sells in its stores in China. Despite challenges in supplier onboarding and data accuracy, Food Trust showcases blockchain's potential to transform food safety and transparency, setting new standards for the industry. This addressed the challenge of not only having a significantly reduced time in detecting an outbreak of a food-borne disease but also identifying the source.

Maersk and IBM's TradeLens

Similar to the above case study, Maersk and IBM developed TradeLens, which is intended to be a blockchain-based shipping platform to digitize the global supply chain and not just the food-related market. Unfortunately, despite developing what appeared to be a viable platform, the initiative was discontinued as TradeLens has failed to achieve the commercial success required to sustain this operation. The intention of Tradelens is to have real-time tracking of cargo and documents, reducing administrative processes and enhancing transparency.

6.5.3. Healthcare

MedicalChain

The Medicalchain[17] platform is based on Hyperledger Fabric blockchain technology that facilitates a "peer-to-peer" network to share electronic health records (EHRs) between patients and clinicians. It grants permission to the patients to allow the free flow of their health data by placing them at the center of their

---

17. Medicalchain Whitepaper. Medicalchain. Accessed September 8, 2024. https://medicalchain.com/Medicalchain-Whitepaper-EN.pdf.

health records and empowering them to control who has access to their health information. Active participation in this long-term medical record is through patient-controlled authenticated access and selective granting of access using a permission system deployed on the blockchain. By employing fully encrypted, immutable records, the system provides transparency and privacy to not only patients but also general practitioners and consultants (for instance, the right to view lab test results, etc). Medicalchain aims to streamline the transfer of patients' health data from one hospital or GP to another while eliminating any form of data silos. The encrypted electronic health record system deployed with blockchain will potentially improve patient outcomes by enabling secure telemedicine consultations while enhancing the security of the data. Medicalchain acknowledges the challenges it faces concerning regulatory compliance and adoption by healthcare entities or regulatory bodies.

MediLedger

MediLedger, hosted on the Quorum blockchain, improves the pharmaceutical supply chain by both increasing regulatory compliance and preventing the distribution of counterfeit drugs. The app ensures that information on products is recorded transparently and securely from manufacture to sale, making it easier to comply with the Drug Supply Chain Security Act (DSCSA), and increasing the efficiency of supply chain processes such as inventory and shipping by allowing data collection and analytic automation through smart contracts. Although some pilots have stalled due to participant concerns around data accuracy, network integrity, and time commitment, results from pioneering companies like Pfizer and Novartis are promising. As the app continues to be developed, it will also simplify the traceability of recalls, which benefits consumers' health, completion of new drug trials, manufacturer profit margins, and reputation. Overall, MediLedger demonstrates the tremendous potential of blockchain to radically improve the effectiveness and regulatory compliance of the pharmaceutical supply chain.

6.5.4. Real Estate

Propy

Propy is using the Ethereum blockchain to create a real estate escrow platform that can help international transactions run more smoothly and safely by automating parts of the process, making the system more transparent, and consequently reducing the potential for fraud. Through the platform, real estate transactions can become faster and less expensive by digitizing the deal and enabling access to the same data from any part of the world, on hammered blockchain, forever. Propy has already carried out multiple successful international real estate deals and has partnered with a few local cities and governments to use its blockchain-backed notarization of deeds to help streamline the process by which property titles both can and should change ownership. Even if the regulations have not yet made these applications widely available, new technology is breaking barriers every day, and it is the responsibility of our society to prepare to embrace the new regime as it unfolds. Regulatory compliance, legal recognition of blockchain-based transactions, and user adoption are some of the hurdles Propy faces currently.

Ubitquity

Ubitquity is another blockchain solution for improving the security, transparency, and efficiency of real estate transactions. Property titles and deeds are allocated to immutable ledgers using Bitcoin and Ethereum, to prevent fraud, ensure the accuracy of verification, and automate processes, ultimately reducing intermediary parties and saving money. The system is designed to streamline record-keeping, which is the core activity of a land registry, and to improve the trustworthiness and ease of scrutiny by end-users, such as lawyers and real estate agents. This use case proves particularly helpful in developing nations, where record-keeping systems are notoriously unreliable.

6.5.5. Government and Public Services

Dubai Blockchain Strategy

Dubai's Blockchain Strategy seeks to transform Dubai into the world's first blockchain-powered government by digitizing every visa application, bill payment, and license renewal using platforms such as Ethereum and Hyperledger Fabric. The strategy aims to improve government efficiency by streamlining processes and reducing paperwork while delivering better economic growth by providing a more conducive environment for innovative new business models to flourish. It also improves transactional security by creating tamper-proof records and ensures transparency through the automation of contracts and embeddedness rules in program code that cannot be altered. Real-world applications could include a blockchain-based land registry, digital identities, and unified health records, all of which would help close the gap between the functions of a government and the needs of its citizens.

Estonia's e-Residency Program

Estonia's e-Residency program, launched in 2014, provides global entrepreneurs with a secure digital identity underpinned by the KSI Blockchain and enables them to register and manage firms in Estonia entirely online. KSI is a blockchain technology designed in Estonia and used globally to ensure networks, systems, and data are free of compromise, all while retaining 100% data privacy. E-residents have access to Estonian banking, and the ability to digitally sign documents, which facilitates and reduces the costs of operations. E-Residency is particularly suited to startups, SMEs, freelancers, and digital nomads, and it offers a stable legal and financial framework supporting global business. Providing access to e-government services in a digital environment improves the overall economic performance. E-Residency shows how blockchain can transform digital governance and international business.

6.5.6. Energy Sector

Power Ledger

Power Ledger is an Australian technology company that applies blockchain to help consumers buy and sell excess solar energy using P2P energy trading. The company applies Ethereum to execute real-time transactions and automated smart contracts in a network, which can decentralize and automate the energy market, while also improving grid efficiency. In the cities of Fremantle in Australia and Bangkok in Thailand, these projects have proven to result in substantial cost savings for consumers and increased use of renewable energy sources. Power Ledger illustrates what blockchain might be able to achieve for energy owners, traders, and consumers: the democratization of the energy market can help consumers take back control from large utilities, and thus reduce pollution, prevent climate change, and promote sustainable renewable energy. Power Ledger highlights several significant challenges for blockchain to transform energy markets and other sectors. These are regulatory, scalability, and integration.

WePower

Built upon the Ethereum blockchain, WePower tokenizes renewable energy allowing the trading and issuance of green energy as digital assets. The production of any given amount of energy is transferred into a tradable digital asset using smart contracts. The energy is thereafter offered to the market where consumers and investors can pre-purchase energy before it is produced by renewable green projects. When an estimated bill is to be paid, it is settled through the blockchain to eliminate any fees and time delays between the buyer and the seller. By using blockchain technology, a peer-to-peer marketplace is created in which all transactions have their immutable records on the blockchain. This enhances liquidity in the market and adds additional levels of transparency to the trading. By extension, the use of WePower accelerates settlement and reduces transaction costs. Regulation, adoption, and integration pose challenges, yet the foregoing explorations show how blockchain can be a transformative technology for energy financing and trading. Small blockchain future exchanges and renewable energy companies such as WePower offer possibilities that were previously unheard of.

6.6 Hyperledger

So far, we have a decent idea of what and how to prepare for a project involving blockchain. In this section, we will introduce Hyperledger in detail and talk about the various projects that are in the scope of the Hyperledger foundation. Hyperledger is not a single blockchain but rather an umbrella project that hosts several distributed ledger frameworks and tools. Each framework within the Hyperledger project may have different characteristics and use cases, and they may implement various consensus mechanisms.

The projects under the Hyperledger foundation are:

1. Fabric
2. Solang
3. Iroha
4. Indy
5. Firefly
6. Cello
7. Caliper
8. Cacti
9. Bevel
10. Besu
11. Aries
12. Identus

We will introduce the most popular of these projects in the following section in brief, to give a glimpse of the different aspects and use cases these projects host.

6.6.1 Hyperledger Fabric

Hyperledger Fabric, developed by IBM for enterprise-level use, is an open-source distributed ledger platform. Described as "open, proven, enterprise-grade DLT" (distributed ledger technology, or blockchain), the platform offers a modular architecture suitable for various applications. One of its notable features is the capability to establish a "network of networks," providing flexibility in ensuring security for transactions involving multiple parties. Unlike a public blockchain, participants in Hyperledger Fabric are known and vetted by a trusted authority, such as a business network founded on a relationship of trust. This permissioned blockchain is suitable for business applications where trust, security, and transparency are paramount. Hyperledger Fabric has a very well-documented manual[18] covering the installation setup, tutorials, commands, architecture, and answers to frequently asked questions. While this book will not get into the details of every aspect of Hyperledger Fabric due to the technical expertise involved in implementing one.

Fabric uses Chaincode which is analogous to smart contracts in Ethereum, to handle business logic agreed to by the members of the network. Chaincode can be written in the same general-purpose programming languages as server software in a traditional distributed application: Go, Java, and Node.js. Fabric uses a Membership Service Provider (MSP) to register individual identities. An MSP handles user authentication, ensuring that participants are who they claim to be, and provides credentials for transaction signing and verification.

6.6.2 Solang

Hyperledger Solang is a bespoke Solidity compiler that lets you use the familiarity and ubiquity of Solidity-based smart contract creation on Solana, and Substrate blockchain ecosystems. For developers familiar with Ethereum's development environment, Solang provides both familiarity and potential for growth on the

---

18. Hyperledger Fabric Documentation. "Welcome to Hyperledger Fabric Documentation,". https://hyperledger-fabric.readthedocs.io/en/latest/index.html.

Solana and Substrate ecosystems. It's an Ethereum development compiler that converts Solidity code to the native bytecode of Solana and Substrate blockchains, so it can be deployed and executed on these blockchains using the base functions and network effects of full nodes.

There are several benefits to Hyperledger Solang, including its support for interoperability between blockchain ecosystems. Thanks to Solidity, which is extremely popular for infrastructure in the Ethereum ecosystem, Solang migrates developers to Solana and Substrate who otherwise may have had to restart all their work from scratch because of the programming language differences. This coding wizardry not only helps the two ecosystems become more inclusive but also reduces the time and resources needed to scale up for bigger projects with wider appeal.

Solana is an accelerated blockchain for building dynamic and fast decentralized applications requiring immense processing power and speed. For these use cases, Solang comes in handy as it allows developers to easily move the existing Solidity contracts on Solana to take advantage of its ultra-high rate and tiny-latency capabilities. Similarly, on Substrate, Solang enhances the flexible and customizable nature of the "toolkit" for building blockchains, where developers can leverage these tools while coding on their spreadsheet editor to reduce coding overhead and elevate productivity, alongside maintaining seamless compatibility with their existing Solidity code.

Furthermore, Hyperledger Solang maintains a 1:1 representation with all Solidity features, including complex data structures, inheritance, and function overloading, enabling the implementation of more advanced logic without compromise within smart contracts. Integration with Solana and Substrate development tooling enables compiling, deploying, and debugging smart contracts – ensuring that developers have a toolchain that can support the entire process of building, testing, and optimizing an application.

All in all, Hyperledger Solang is an indispensable tool for developers wishing to port their Solidity-based smart contracts to Solana and Substrate, as well as to Ethereum, thanks to its ability to interconnect different blockchain ecosystems. With its support for full Solidity features and ever-growing integration with native toolchains, Solang represents a valuable addition to the blockchain development ecosystem. By democratizing the Porting process and unifying smart-contract development, Solang encourages the development of new decentralized applications, fostering blockchain innovation, and enhancing interoperability, eventually driving the decentralized Internet revolution.

6.6.3 Iroha

Hyperledger Iroha is a blockchain framework created by the Hyperledger project that simplifies the development of secure, scalable, and easy-to-use distributed ledger applications. The focus of the design was ease of implementation to provide a simple and convenient end-user experience. Because of this focus on usability, this framework is designed for enterprise environments and is written in C++ for performance. One of the features is Yet Another Consensus (YAC), an algorithm that supports Byzantine fault tolerance and provides full finality for a transaction and fault tolerance.

Using the built-in Iroha commands and queries, saying things like 'pay 10 gold to Alice' or 'Mark Tomas's rep_pay period as +1', one can specify or respond to actions in the network. This lowers the barrier of entry for developers, allowing them to work with assets, identities, and data instead of worrying about underlying dry blockchain technology. Logically, one can also specify and revoke access rules with fine-grained controls, so that not everyone but only certain people (based on signatures) would be authorized to do those actions. If privacy and compliance are vital for your enterprise applications, then Iroha's access control would help maintain that.

Because Hyperledger Iroha has a modular architecture, it is straightforward to integrate with other systems and frameworks in the Hyperledger suite. One notable use case is that Hyperledger Iroha supports multi-signature transactions – a way of safeguarding operation-critical transactions by requiring multiple signatures, and has a simple API that makes it easier to integrate with any existing business processes and systems. This can be an appealing approach for enterprises looking to leverage blockchain technology without major operational changes.

As such, Hyperledger Iroha has been used in the financial, healthcare, and supply chain management industries, to deal with digital assets that require performance and reliability. For instance: in the financial sector, Iroha could be used to manage digital currencies and tokens. In healthcare, patient records and data sharing between institutions can be managed by Iroha. This provides more efficient and secure use of such data. Due to its wide scope, ease of use, high simplicity, good security, modular design, and flexibility, Hyperledger Iroha is an excellent candidate as a blockchain framework for enterprises.

6.6.4 Indy

Hyperledger Indy is the world's first open-source, distributed ledger-based identity system. It enables individuals, organizations, and Internet of Things (IoT) smart devices to establish a secure digital identity using self-sovereign credentials that are private, tamper-proof, and carry proof of authority, without relying on third-party identity providers to establish proof of existence. Customers and IoT identities can freely create, store, manage, and update unique digital identities, using distributed ledger technology to securely define, store, and control their identities. Indy enables an electronic 'Know Your Customer' (KYC) process that takes place in a distributed ledger where a group of independently operated nodes administers the identity of each user rather than a centralized authority.

Hyperledger Indy is anchored around other fundamental technologies like verifiable credentials – cryptographic attestations issued by a trusted source proving an individual's identity/ attributes, which may be presented and verified in a privacy-preserving manner without the individual having to divulge their entire identity or expose other sensitive data. This guarantees online anonymity and security, which any user would prioritize to prevent the risk of data leaks and identity theft. The service provider doesn't store or share sensitive data, instead offering certain services such as performing validity checks on queries, in a manner where the user explicitly determines when to share this information or with whom. Hyperledger Indy includes specifications for self-sovereign identity (SSI), where one can own and control their own digital identity. SSI empowers users to collect credentials from several separate sources (for instance: education, work, and banking) and manage them all in a distributed way so that they have a unified, interoperable, and pervasive identity experience across various platforms and services. The SSI capability is especially useful in a digital world where a user interacts with many organizations and service providers, each requiring identity validation.

The architecture of Hyperledger Indy consists of the following layers and components:

- The Indy Ledger is a public, permissioned blockchain based on Hyperledger Fabric, holding Decentralized Identifiers(DIDs) and public keys – the identity data is immutable and available for normal queries.

- The Indy Wallet can be installed on a device for private key storage, digital credentials management, and other sensitive information. It allows users to create their DIDs and have control over their digital identities.

- The Indy Agent, which expands the capabilities of the wallet, serves as an interface for the wallet to interact with other entities in the Indy network, enabling users to share verifiable credentials with a receiver upon request.

Hyperledger Indy provides a new model for identity management that advances security, privacy, and self-sovereignty for users. With an eye to scalability and interoperability, Indy integrates digital IDs as verifiable credentials in a decentralized ledger technology. By adhering to a self-sovereign identity standard and backed by an open-source network of global businesses, universities, and national governments, Indy will both scale the needs for government verification and fulfill the SSIs for future businesses and workforce.

Key-Terms

Compliance	Fabric	Hyperledger	Integration
Interoperability	Project-planning	Sidechains	State-channels
Testing			

Quiz

1. Considering a project that is involved with high-volume and high-frequency transactions, why might a blockchain not be a good fit?

   a. Blockchain systems typically have slower transaction speeds.

   b. Blockchain systems are too expensive.

   c. Blockchain systems are too complex.

   d. Blockchain systems are not secure.

2. Which of the following would you consider as the primary focus of the initial planning phase for a blockchain project?

   a. Coding the blockchain

   b. Marketing the blockchain

   c. Establishing clear objectives and potential use cases

   d. Hiring developers

3. When a blockchain project is implemented in a supply chain industry, it is typically done for one of the following reasons:

   a. Improving the user interface

   b. Reducing fraud by adding traceability

   c. Increasing the number of employees

   d. Launching a marketing campaign

4. Given the popularity of blockchain, over the last decade, we can argue that blockchain can be a solution to every problem out there.

   a. True

   b. False

5. Which blockchain platform is known for its permissioned network and strong privacy features?

   a. Ethereum

   b. Hyperledger Fabric

   c. Polkadot

   d. Bitcoin

6. The blockchain that is designed specifically for financial services and focuses on privacy is:

   a. Ethereum

   b. Hyperledger Fabric

   c. R3 Corda

   d. Quorum

7. Sidechains have a purpose in blockchain integration, which is:

   a. to increase transaction fees

   b. to scale blockchains and increase interoperability

   c. to slow down transaction speeds

   d. to decrease security

8. The type of testing that is focused on ensuring different components or services work together as intended is called _____.

   a. unit testing

   b. security testing

   c. integration testing

   d. performance testing

9. Which tool is used for performance testing in Hyperledger Fabric?

   a. MythXf

   b. Hyperledger Composer

   c. Hyperledger Caliper

   d. Truffle

10. Which of the following best describes Quorum?

   a. A public blockchain developed by J.P. Morgan

   b. A cryptocurrency exchange platform

   c. An enterprise-variant of Ethereum developed by J.P. Morgan

   d. A stablecoin used for international transactions

Answers	1 – a	2 – c	3 – b	4 – b	5 – b
	6 – c	7 – b	8 – c	9 – c	10 – c

Chapter Summary

◆ Successful blockchain projects start by defining clear objectives and conducting a rigorous feasibility study to assess the technical, economic, and operational viability and appropriateness of blockchain

◆ The key to choosing the right blockchain is to compare blockchain types, consensus mechanisms, market solutions, costs, legal requirements, and the community that supports the best option for your project's goals.

◆ Integrating blockchain into a legacy system improves transparency, security, and efficiency while showcasing new opportunities for innovation and compliance.

◆ A successful blockchain project depends on thorough testing and careful deployment strategies.

◆ Hyperledger is an umbrella project that hosts several frameworks and tools related to blockchain.

◆ Chaincode in Hyperledger Fabric is analogous to smart contracts in Ethereum.

Chapter 7

The Future of Blockchain

In the previous chapters of this book, we started building the basic infrastructure of blockchain as well as reading about the types of blockchain and cryptocurrencies and how to transfer funds to the intended recipient. Most importantly, we looked into the glimpse of creating a smart contract along with deploying a private blockchain. In the closing chapter of our book, we are going to explore the future of blockchain, more importantly:

- Distributed government networks – how can blockchain play a crucial role in the government?

- Dangers of blockchain – what are the potential limitations or implications of blockchain?

- Exploring the rise of blockchain – Unveiling emerging markets and their potential impact on the global landscape.

- Leverages of blockchain – Where is blockchain being put into use?

- After blockchain – Web4? Web5?

> After studying the final chapter, you should be able to:
>
> - Understand the potential dangers of blockchain
>
> - Explain the concept of the Virtual Blockchain World (VBW)
>
> - Determine the various ways in which the blockchain can be leveraged
>
> - Grasp the future of blockchain

7.1 Decentralized World, Distributed Government, and Multilevel Networks

Given the hack-resistant system that blockchain boasts of, imagine a scalable, quantum-resistant* system allowing you to virtually access your desktop and digital content from any computer in the world. There have been many such prototypes generated over the last few years. Decentraland, Somnium Space, Nexus, and Cryptovexels are a few examples of that architecture, where a virtual space can be owned and traded for money. These architectures are often referred to as Virtual Blockchain World (VBW). Metaverse is a step above the VBW, given that Metaverse is a digital ecosystem built on various kinds of 3D technology, real-time collaboration software, and blockchain technologies. Let's discuss VBW a little more in detail as this will play a major role in the future of blockchain.

7.1.1 Virtual Blockchain World (VBW)

VBW, short for Virtual Blockchain World, are social platforms in which lands/properties are owned by players, companies, or investors. These lands/properties that are hinted at earlier are not physical places, but just virtual spaces. These virtual spaces can be seen when logged into the VBW. Anybody can rent or own the land giving them the right to build whatever they want to. The land can also be seen as a real estate market where one can sell their land to other users for profit. You can walk around your purchased land with your avatar in the game/app and build anything you want upon it.

Cryptocurrency will be used to purchase the land in VBW, which is done using Metamask. Not only can you build your land/ assets on the VBW but you can also interact with other people in the virtual world. Usually, the goal of such worlds is for the users to have a fun experience. In short, Decentraland is a software that seeks to give a global network of users incentives to operate a shared virtual world.

Fun Fact

Decentraland is the largest VBW in the market right now, and it received funding of more than $26 million through ICO in August 2017. As of now, this particular VBW does not have any support for virtual reality

Traditionally, in a VBW, everything you purchase is represented by NFT. The NFT is used to represent true ownership of a unique asset on the blockchain, and in the case of VBW, it could range from land/property/asset. Ultimately, the usage of NFT depends on the VBW. Another way of representing an NFT is looking at them as digital collectibles, where each collectible comes in various forms such as game items, sports memorabilia, digital land, event tickets, or even a tweet and much more (all of this within the VBW).

7.2 The Dangers of Blockchain

Introducing something new into the financial market is going to take time, especially when, on average, the total money transactions per day is more than $4.5 trillion. Blockchain offers a significant advantage in facilitating global fund transfers with minimal fees, in contrast to fiat currency, where transaction fees often constitute a percentage of the total amount. Additionally, blockchain has the potential to circumvent restrictions imposed by governments or limitations due to lack of accessibility. Despite this significant advantage, it's important to consider potential risks associated with blockchain technology. This section looks into the potential dangers of blockchain architecture and its use cases. Some of them are the ability to:

- Turn off

- Erase

- Retrieve private key once lost

- Dispute

- Consume less energy

- Prove a decentralization system

7.2.1 Distributed control

By now, we have established that blockchain is a distributed database without any central authority. Blockchain runs on thousands of nodes depending on the architecture and popularity. The advantage of this distributed feature is that financial transactions can be validated and verified without a third party. This distributed feature might also work against the blockchain as there is no on/off switch to turn off the blockchain, unlike centralized servers which could be turned off when an attack or a defect is detected in the system.

This ability of not being able to turn off the blockchain can be looked upon as one of the potential dangers of this architecture. There have been many incidents where hackers have found flaws in the code of the blockchain. The flaw could be in the source code of the blockchain itself, a major flaw in the smart contracts, or one that exploits a bug in the programming language.

Out of the many such incidents that occurred in the past, the cryptocurrency exchange wallets are the ones that are highly targeted. There were more than 25 cryptocurrency exchange breaches in 2020, totaling more than $300 million in loss – that's an average of $10.72 million per hack. In 2017, hackers exploited the open coding of the Ethereum blockchain platform to siphon away millions of dollars. But once they were on the trail of the misused bug, no one was able to shut it down, because blockchain doesn't have an off switch. On a similar note, if anyone can find a bug in the software, they might be able to exploit it before anyone else notices and fixes it.

7.2.2 Cannot delete!

Another supposed advantage of blockchain is that, once you put the transaction onto the blockchain, you cannot effectively remove that transaction, and everyone else on the blockchain can see all the transactions that have ever taken place. Although this might sound like a very huge advantage, what if there are things stored on the blockchain which should never be visible to the general public?

One of the use cases of blockchain is in the voting process which can be achieved through a smart contract. Consider an example where there is a smart contract that is used for voting purposes that takes in the details of the user. What if the smart contract mistakenly publishes the user's details onto the blockchain? This could lead to identities being stolen without a way to prevent it.

Another example is to imagine a scenario where blockchain is being used to store criminal records. Many states in the US and also countries around the world offer expunging of a criminal record depending on the crimes. If the criminal records are written onto the blockchain, later on in the future it would be impossible for the terminal to expunge that record. Numerous illustrations of this nature underscore the dual nature of the inability to delete in the blockchain, presenting both advantages and disadvantages.

7.2.3 Lose your key, lose everything!

A blockchain account can be accessed using a private key. If the private key is lost or falls into the hands of someone else, it is impossible to retrieve the account. There have been many real-life examples of users who have lost private keys worth millions of dollars. There is no stopping someone trying to impersonate you if they get a hold of your key.

7.2.4 Dispute

Fraud transactions that are made on your credit card or debit card can be disputed with the bank/financial organization that issued the card. The dispute will be taken to court if necessary but can be resolved either way. No such dispute transactions can be raised on transactions made on blockchain because there is no central authority. This disadvantage of not being able to raise disputes is another potential danger of using blockchain.

7.2.5 Energy consumption

As of 2023, the amount of electricity used for Bitcoin on average per year is more than in countries like Chile, Denmark, Norway, and so on. The amount of energy needed to post one transaction on Bitcoin is equivalent to the energy used by an American household for two months. This underscores the substantial ongoing research efforts aimed at transitioning blockchain to utilize a more advanced consensus algorithm. Efforts are being made to utilize the energy being wasted, especially in wind farms.[19]

---

19. Dorrell, John; Kancharla, Abhilash; Ambrosia, Matthew (2024). John Dorrell, Abhilash Kancharla, and Matthew Ambrosia, "Green Crypto Mining: A Quantitative Analysis of the Profitability of Bitcoin Mining Using Excess Wind Energy," The Journal of Energy and Development, vol. 48, no. 1 (copyright 2023), pp. 1–22.. figshare. Journal contribution. https://doi.org/10.6084/m9.figshare.25055597.v1.

7.2.6 Is it really decentralized?

The current group of miners in Bitcoin are the ones that have very specialized mining rigs. As the number of blocks increases in Bitcoin, the hash rate* also increases. The increase in the hash rate demands even better equipment to mine the blockchain. Eventually, this will result in only a very few groups being able to afford the necessary mining equipment, thus, reducing the factor of decentralization. To solve this problem, cryptocurrencies will have to come up with creative solutions.

7.3 Leveraging blockchain

Blockchain is currently one of those buzzwords that every business leader and techie likes to deploy when discussing the next big thing. Blockchain can be leveraged as a base to build the financial system to fill the gaps in the online market. Blockchain is being considered to see if it's a good fit for almost every technology out there. There are many ways blockchain is being leveraged, other than just cryptocurrency. Given how fast the technology is changing, this section will look into the different ways of leveraging blockchain in detail:

7.3.1 Banking

Before we dive into how blockchain can be leveraged in the banking industry, let's look at the difference in the transaction fees in Bitcoin vs Banks. The major difference is that in Bitcoin, the transaction fees are flat, meaning regardless of the amount of transactions, the Bitcoin fee is fixed per transaction unlike the traditional third-party vendors like VISA and Mastercard wherein the fee is a percentage of the total amount of a transaction. The higher the amount being transferred, the higher the transaction fee in banks. For blockchain, the transaction fee remains the same regardless of the amount. For higher amounts, blockchain will be much cheaper compared to banks. In conclusion, numerous factors warrant careful consideration before forming opinions on banks or blockchains. Some of them include:

- The sender can wait for transactions to be posted to the blockchain. The time to post a transaction on Bitcoin can take anywhere between seconds to 60 minutes.

- The sender doesn't need to use fiat currency.

- The receiver also has access to funds sent by the sender.

7.3.2 Government

Blockchain and Government might not look like a good fit together; however, blockchain technology can be ideal for recording and preserving data that can be safe to be put out in public. The majority of countries have a voting system to elect someone to run the government.

1. Blockchain can play a major role in the voting procedure for the government. Ballot boxes used for voting can be completely revolutionized using the concept of smart contracts. This ensures no margin of duplication or tampering with a vote. Not only that but it also ensures that the statistics of the voting are revealed to the public without any ambiguity. Another advantage of voting through smart contracts is that people can choose to vote from their devices like a laptop or a mobile rather than coming in person.

2. Because credentials are dispersed among thousands of computers on a permissioned blockchain instead of residing on a single server, the risk of hacking is greatly reduced. In 2017, Equifax, a global credit reporting and analytics agency reported that the personal information of some 147 million people had been transferred following a security breach.

3. Governments are always looking for some centralized cloud-type infrastructure that could check the documents of every citizen in their country and, perhaps, blockchain could deliver that. Rather than storing any relevant information on the public blockchain, the government could use the hash value of the documents. This would allow the provision of attested and permanently time-stamped versions of the documents.

4. Using smart contracts, the government can track the ownership and transfers of an asset like land, property, or vehicle. This transfer of ownership can be made public without revealing any personal details. This will make it a lot easier for the government to validate the proof of ownership too.

7.3.3 Education

Blockchain technology holds great potential to revolutionize the education sector. Security is the most obvious and widely discussed use of blockchain, ensuring that diplomas and certificates cannot be falsely claimed. Storing student records on a decentralized, transparent blockchain can also guarantee privacy and greater security for the individual's record than a centralized system would. The use of smart contracts can automate aspects of administration, such as the process of enrolling in a course and paying the fees. Because it can encompass many different alphanumeric characters, it can be used to issue nuanced micro-credentials, allowing students to earn badges for the information they provide, the questions they answer, or the projects they complete. Additionally, the technology can foster decentralized learning platforms, enabling direct content sharing between educators and students.

Blockchain's role extends to collaborative research, where it ensures the integrity of research data and publications. Moreover, it facilitates global student mobility by simplifying the transfer of academic credits between institutions, promoting a seamless and verifiable process. Blockchain can be used to verify the digital identity of students and faculty, thereby making the personal information of individuals who learn and teach more secure. The applications of this technology will ultimately expand in education, and likely usher in a new mode of efficiency, transparency, and security.

7.3.4 Supply chain

Because most of the products nowadays tend to come from citizens of different countries, with more than one stopping point in a supply chain, it has become much more complex to track or make the chain transparent and more efficient. Customers will have clarity on where the product originated and how it was distributed. Using blockchain in the supply chain industry will:

1. Improve tracking and transparency, for both the supplier and the intermediary parties as well as the end customer.

2. Promote more ethical and sustainable methods of production and distribution. With the help of smart contracts, deadlines can be programmed within the smart contract.

3. Make payments easier, if the entire transaction is made using cryptocurrency.

4. Zero out the single-point failure issues. Potential issues in the process of the supply chain can be tracked by every single party in that supply chain.

7.3.5 IoT

Internet of Things (IoT) is a buzzword to denote the network of physical objects equipped with sensors, processing ability, software, and other technologies to connect and exchange data over a network. As IoT devices have their identities, those identities can be used on private blockchain networks to send and receive the data to create an immutable record, which is not vulnerable to tampering. With the help of blockchain, IoT device transactions can be trusted, and trust is one of the main characteristics that blockchain boasts of. The combination of blockchain and IoT facilitates provenance tracking in supply chain management, secure identity and access management for devices, tokenization of IoT-generated data for fair exchange, and the automation of agreements through smart contracts. Additionally, blockchain enables novel applications such as peer-to-peer energy trading in smart grids and decentralized governance models for IoT networks. In general, IoT and blockchain technology together in synergy present solutions driven by the need for improved security and transparency, as well as overall increased efficiency in various scenarios of digitization.

New terms so far

- **Quantum-resistant:** Because quantum computers can potentially destroy certain cryptographic algorithms, it is important to implement cryptography in ways that are "quantum-safe". It is important for cryptographic protocols, which are used to secure information on today's computers, to be replaced as quantum computing technology becomes available.

- **Hash Rate:** Hash rate is a measure of the amount of hashes that a mining machine or network of machines performs per second. Hashrate is typically measured in hashes per second (H/s), kilohashes per second (KH/s), megahashes per second (MH/s), gigahashes per second (GH/s), or even terahashes per second (TH/s), depending on the scale of the mining operation.

7.4 What's next for blockchain?

Blockchain entered the financial industry with the sole purpose of cryptocurrencies. Then the smart contracts were born (Ethereum) and introduced into the blockchain ecosystem, which subsequently increased the number of use cases of blockchain. As stated before, there are a lot of uncertainties about blockchain platforms and it will take time for blockchain to be standardized. Many new consensus algorithms have created alternate ways to validate and at the same time, utilize as few resources as possible. Hence, the future of blockchain is set on creating much more efficient ways of utilizing the technology.

Blockchain games have also been showing a considerable rise in the market. Typically, blogs and games are the first things that come to mind when thinking of cryptocurrencies and NFTs. In-game items or assets have "real world" value, implying that such an item/asset can be sold for money. In 2021, the Valve Corporation blocked blockchain games from its distribution platform – Steam. This block is an extension of the rules that previously banned any game on Steam offering items with real-world value.

Although blockchain is still an emerging technology, it is spreading at a fast pace. Many of the drawbacks of blockchain require to be amended, including scalability, energy requirement, privacy, and others. Unless and until these limitations are catered to, blockchain will not be able to climb higher up in the technology market. Developing the right tools/architecture to address these limitations will take time, just like how the internet took a lot of time to get settled and become what we use right now. Given the technological advancements happening around the globe surrounding blockchain, there is a high chance that blockchain will be commonplace in the near future just like how the internet is at the moment. The fast-paced changes in technological advancements make it even harder to guess what's in the future for the blockchain, but one thing is for sure — blockchain will pave the path for upcoming technologies. It will take a generation or two for the advancement of technology from Web3 to Web4.

Key-Terms

Decentraland	Decentralized	IoT	Metaverse
NFT	VBW		

Quiz

1. **IoT stands for:**

   a. Internet of Things

   b. Internet of Tasks

   c. Intranet of Things

   d. Intranet of Tasks

2. **In cryptocurrency, the transaction fee remains the same regardless of the amount.**

   a. True

   b. False

3. _____ **is a process involved in the production and distribution of a commodity typically, from a supplier to an end customer.**

   a. Smart contracting

   b. Supply chain

   c. Transportation

   d. Transaction

4. **What is the term used for social platforms where virtual lands can be owned and traded?**

    a. Virtual Land Platforms

    b. Crypto Spaces

    c. Virtual Blockchain Worlds (VBW)

    d. Cryptovexels Platforms

5. **A blockchain can be turned on and off in an instant.**

    a. True

    b. False

6. **What are the advantages of blockchain?**

    a. Minimal transaction fees

    b. No third-party financial service

    c. Smart contracts

    d. All of the above

7. **Blockchain is used to trace a product from the supplier to the end consumer in the supply chain industry.**

    a. True

    b. False

8. **One of the below can be categorized as a potential danger of blockchain.**

    a. Centralized control

    b. Ability to delete transactions

    c. Energy consumption

    d. Ability to turn off the blockchain

9. **VBW in blockchain stands for:**

    a. Virtual Blockchain Work

    b. Virtual Block World

    c. Virtual Blockchain World

    d. None of the above

10. **The limitations of blockchain are:**

    a. Scalability

    b. High energy usage

    c. Privacy

    d. All of the above

Answers	1 – a	2 – a	3 – b	4 – c	5 – b
	6 – d	7 – a	8 – c	9 – c	10 – d

Chapter Summary

◆ While blockchain seems to be a foolproof mechanism, there are many underlying potential dangers.

◆ Extensive research needs to be done in the area of blockchain to cover up all the flaws, which creates more use cases for blockchain.

◆ A Virtual Blockchain World (VBW) is a virtual world that runs on blockchain.

◆ Blockchain is currently being explored for potential use across various public and private sectors